I0793828

PRAYERS *for Every Season*

More Common Prayer for Children and Families

TIMOTHY J. S. SEAMANS

Church PUBLISHING

Copyright © 2024 by Timothy J. S. Seamans

All rights reserved. No part of this book may be reproduced, stored in a retrieval system, or transmitted in any form or by any means, electronic or mechanical, including photo- copying, recording, or otherwise, without the written permission of the publisher. Unless otherwise noted, the Scripture quotations are from New Revised Standard Version Bible, copyright © 1989 National Council of the Churches of Christ in the United States of America. Used by permission. All rights reserved worldwide.

Church Publishing
19 East 34th Street
New York, NY 10016
www.churchpublishing.org

Cover art by Perry Hodgkins Jones
Cover design by Newgen
Typeset by Nord Compo

Library of Congress Control Number: 2024931168
ISBN 978-1-64065-665-9 (paperback)
ISBN 978-1-64065-666-6 (eBook)

CONTENTS AT A GLANCE

TABLE OF CONTENTS

FOREWORD
Jenifer Gamber

As people made in the image of God, children are born with the divine spark shining within. Christians call this spark the light of Christ. This divine spark animates children's innate curiosity and frames how they experience the world. Children approach the world with an expectation that the world is saturated with meaning, purpose, and direction. For children, the world is enchanted, demanding from us a stance of wonder. God's love and desire is present in every moment of life.

As caregivers of children, we bear a responsibility to cultivate this wonder, openness to mystery, and natural connection with God. This responsibility is particularly important in a world that increasingly tells us, and our children, that nothing lies behind the world that we see. The divine spark will always be a part of each person. But, just as muscles can atrophy when not exercised, this light within can lose its guiding power and ability to animate how we understand ourselves and the world when not affirmed or given the opportunity to express itself.

When children are affirmed in their innate understanding of a world saturated with God's goodness, God's love and a world of possibilities opens.

Timothy has learned about the reality of the divine spark from firsthand experience with his own children and the many children in his care as a school chaplain. God indeed has been speaking to every child from before they were born.

This book of prayers provides a tool for parents and caregivers to join the conversation our children are already having with God. You will find prayers for the morning and evening and for special days throughout the year—both in the Church and in the world.

Have this book on hand at your kitchen table and on your child's nightstand. Let your children thumb through its pages and color the fanciful characters. Noticing the illustrations will enliven their imaginations and help them enter the prayers beyond the words.

Many of the prayers are in the form of a conversation, reflecting an understanding that many of the blessings of this world are in the spaces between people. As you pray together, eventually your children will know these words as their own and ground their days in God's enduring love.

Take a moment each day or week and offer the gift that your children bear by affirming a world saturated by the light of Christ through prayer.

INTRODUCTION
"What is prayer?"

Kindergartners often ask me this. I tell them that prayer is the act of connecting our lives to God's love. Common forms of prayer include giving thanks, praying for our own needs and the needs of others, for guidance to make good choices and be kind, for the dead, and for God's presence, especially during times of trial or on special occasions.

I also emphasize something that I did not realize about prayer until I had children of my own. When we're sensitive enough to the light of Christ that's deep within our soul, we find that even before we talk to God in prayer, God is already speaking and having a conversation within us.

Once we listen to what God is already saying, the Holy Spirit draws us into the Son's eternal conversation with the Father. Prayer brings us into the life of the Holy Trinity. We never pray alone.

I have found that the more I pray with others, especially children, the more I grow to realize that angels are always praying around us; the saints are always praying with us and for us; and, in spirit, we are always praying in the company of our fellow Christians on earth and in heaven.

As you use this book, before speaking in prayer, I hope you pause to pay attention to the presence of God and listen to the eternal conversation God is already having within you. You may also be surprised to already know some of the words to this conversation by heart—the words that Jesus taught us also to pray in the Lord's Prayer. These are the same words Christ prays with us now and always. They are the same words Christ has been praying within each of us since before we knew how to pray.

The Lord's Prayer

(traditional)

Our Father who art in heaven,
    hallowed be thy name.
    thy kingdom come,
    thy will be done,
        on earth as it is in heaven.
Give us this day our daily bread.
And forgive us our trespasses,
    as we forgive those who trespass against us.
And lead us not into temptation,
    but deliver us from evil.
For thine is the kingdom and the power and the glory,
    forever and ever. Amen.

(contemporary)

Our Father in heaven,
  hallowed be your Name,
  your kingdom come,
  your will be done,
    on earth as in heaven.
Give us today our daily bread.
Forgive us our sins
  as we forgive those
    who sin against us.
Save us from the time of trial,
  and deliver us from evil.
For the kingdom, the power,
  and the glory are yours,
  now and for ever. Amen.

General Thanksgiving

Living God, firstborn from the dead,
we give you thanks and praise,
for all the blessings of this life,
but above all for your eternal love
revealed through the resurrection of Jesus Christ.
And, we pray, fill us up with so much love,
that with truly thankful hearts
we may share that love with others,
not only with our lips, but in our lives,
by giving up ourselves to your service,
and by walking beside you
in holiness and justice all our days;
through Jesus Christ our Savior,
to whom, with you and the Holy Spirit,
be honor and glory throughout all ages.
Amen.

Prayer for Grace

God of grace,
you open our hearts, know our hopes,
and see our true selves.
Let your Holy Spirit inspire us
to perfectly love you
and to love our neighbors as ourselves.
In Jesus' name we pray.
Amen.

Prayer for Forgiveness

Loving God, we are sorry
for the hurtful things we have thought, said, or done,
and for not doing the things we should have done.
We ask for your forgiveness.
Set us on your way
and make us whole.
Amen.

PART 1

Praying Through the Day

"I wish we could go inside that world," said my student, looking at the towering mural of Christ's nativity inside Grace Cathedral in San Francisco.

Imagine you're also a child standing in front of an immense painting. It covers the wall and is as high as the ceiling. Now imagine the painting is enchanted. Viewers may step inside the painting's world and become part of its story.

This section invites you to enter God's world each morning and evening through prayer, scripture, and daily reflection. Organized by the seasons of the Church Year, each season is like a painting that welcomes you into a major chapter of Jesus Christ's story.

Prayers begin with an awareness that God is always shining within us and inviting us to love. The prayers that follow connect us to the holy people and actions highlighted within the Church's seasons. They prepare us to locate God's presence throughout the day and night.

Scripture is selected for each season with the intention of being read repeatedly. This is best done using a variety of approaches—imagining yourself in the Biblical scene, listening for a word or phrase that speaks to you, wondering about an image or idea, or considering what is left unsaid or implied. The hope is that scripture will come to feel like a world that we can walk around within and discover truths about God and ourselves.

Reflection (my daughter's favorite part of prayer) is where we talk about our experiences of being in God's world. The questions used for reflection are based on the Examen—a Jesuit technique of prayer that invites us to find the movement of God in all the people and events of our day.

Advent – Morning

Opening

Leader: *Our God and Savior now draws near.*
People: *Let us gather in stillness and silence.*

Pause for 10 seconds of holy silence or lighting of the Advent candle.

Leader: *God, open our lips.*
People: *And our mouth shall proclaim your praise.*
All: *Glory to the Holy One: God from God, Light from Light, true God from true God (†): as it was in the beginning, is now, and will be for ever.*
Amen. Alleluia.

Leader: *Let us pray:*
All: *God of grace,*
you open our hearts, know our hopes,
and see our true selves.
Let your Holy Spirit inspire us
to perfectly love you
and to love our neighbors as ourselves.
In Jesus' name we pray.
Amen.

Scripture

And the angel Gabriel said to Mary, "Do not be afraid, for you have found favor with God. And behold, you will become pregnant and bear a son, and you shall call his name Jesus. He will be great and will be called the Son of the Most High. Mary said, "Here I am. I am the Lord's servant, let it be with me according to your word." And then the angel left her.
—Luke 1:30-32, 38 (NRSV adapted)

Invitation

In the season of Advent, we prepare for God's arrival. God came to us as Jesus Christ, and God still arrives in many ways. God comes not just through prayer and worship but through the people we meet and the beauty of creation; through our emotions, ideas, and activities; and through the light shining in our souls. Let us live the questions: "Where will God arrive in my day?" and "How can I let Christ shine through me today?"

Prayers

Let us pray:
God of hope, as the sun rises we trust that Christ rises in our hearts.
God of peace, guide us to follow Jesus down the path of justice.
God of joy, open our eyes to see your light shining today.
God of love, may all who have died rest in your endless light. (†)
For what else shall we pray?

Lord's Prayer

Closing

Leader: *Our God and Savior now draws near.*
People: *Thanks be to God.*

Advent – Evening

Opening

Leader: *O come, O come, Immanuel,*
People: *Immanuel shall come to you, O Israel.*
Leader: *Light and peace, in Jesus Christ our Lord.*
People: *Thanks be to God.*

Advent Collect

God of gifts and surprises, you promised your Son
would come to bring peace on earth and joy to the world.
Like Mary, let us open our lives to the Holy Spirit
and carry the light of Christ into the world.
Like Joseph, let us dream of your arrival.
As we prepare for Jesus to come,
set our hearts on fire with love for you.
Amen.

Scripture

In the last days, God says, I will pour out my Spirit on all people. Your sons and daughters will prophesy. Your young will see visions. Your elders will dream dreams. —Acts 2:17 (CEB)

Reflecting on the Day

- *Who or what are you grateful for today?*
- *Think about your day. What activities did you do? What feelings did you have? What did you notice?*
- *If God was part of your day, share how God arrived.*
- *Describe one way you let the light of Jesus shine through you.*

Confession

Leader: *In the gentle light of Christ, let us confess our sins.*
God of grace, Mary gave her consent to be the mother of Jesus.

People: *Forgive us when we fail to listen and make bad choices.*

Leader: *The magi followed the star to find where Jesus would be born.*

People: *Forgive us when we fail to seek you out.*

Leader: *For all the sins we have done*

People: *and for all the good we have failed to do.*

All: *Forgive and heal us. Amen.*

Prayers

God of hope, keep us safe in our sleep tonight.
God of peace, drive away fears or worries that keep us awake.
Give us joy; speak to us in our dreams.
God of love, give us faith that Christ rests in our hearts.

Lord's Prayer

Closing

Guide us waking, O God, and guard us sleeping,
that awake we may watch with Christ,
and asleep we may rest in peace.
Amen.

Christmas – Morning

Opening

Leader: *Go tell it on the mountain, that Jesus Christ is born.*
People: *Let us gather in stillness and silence.*

Holy silence or lighting of a candle or incense

Leader: *God, open our lips,*
People: *and our mouth shall proclaim your praise.*
All: *Glory to the Father, and to the Son, and to the Holy Spirit: one God and Mother of us all, (†) as it was in the beginning, is now, and ever shall be. World without end. Alleluia.*

Leader: *Let us pray:*
All: *God of grace,*
you open our hearts, know our hopes,
and see our true selves.
Let your Holy Spirit inspire us
to perfectly love you
and to love our neighbors as ourselves.
In Jesus' name we pray.
Amen.

Scripture

Joseph went up out of the city of Nazareth with his wife Mary. Because he was a descendant of King David, they traveled to the city of David, which is called Bethlehem. And so it was that while they were in Bethlehem the day came for Mary's child to be born. She brought forth Jesus, her firstborn son, wrapped him in a blanket, and laid him in a manger, because there was no room for them in the inn. —Luke 2:4-7 (NRSV, adapted)

Invitation

Many people ask, "Where is God?" When Jesus arrives, we learn in the Bible that he will also be called "Immanuel," which means "God with us." Prayer helps us have faith that God is with us. For each of the 12 days of Christmas, take a few moments to pause, pray, and welcome Christ Jesus into your soul. Jesus will help you discover where God is. God is with us.

Prayers

Let us pray:
Wonderful Counselor, give us faith that Christ is born in our hearts.
Mighty God, guide us to follow Jesus down the path of justice.
Prince of Peace, open our eyes to see your light shining today.
Immanuel, may all who have died rest in your endless light. (†)
For what else shall we pray?

Lord's Prayer

Closing

Leader: *Go tell it on the mountain, that Jesus Christ is born.*
People: *Thanks be to God.*

Christmas – Evening

Opening

Leader: *O come, all ye faithful,*
People: *O come, let us adore him.*
Leader: *Light and peace, in Jesus Christ our Lord.*
People: *Thanks be to God.*

Christmas Collect

O God who became human, Word made flesh,
in baby Jesus you arrived as we all do,
needing the love and care of others to survive;
teach us to treasure all babies and children;
help us to know that all bodies are holy,
and that the body of the earth and universe is holy;
and guide us to give special care
to those who are weak, powerless, and most in need of love.
We pray in the name of Immanuel, God with us.
Amen.

Scripture

There were shepherds living out in the fields nearby Bethlehem, keeping watch over their flocks of sheep at night. Suddenly an angel appeared, and the shepherds were badly frightened, but the angel reassured them, "Do not be afraid! I bring you good news of great joy for all people. For a Savior, who is Christ the Lord, is born unto you this day in the town of David. And this will be a sign for you: you will find a baby wrapped in clothes and lying in a manger." —Luke 2:8-12 (NIV, adapted)

Reflecting on the Day

- *Who or what are you grateful for today?*
- *Think about your day. What activities did you do? What feelings did you have? What did you notice?*
- *Looking back at your day, is there any way that God surprised you?*

Confession

Leader: *In the gentle light of Christ, let us confess our sins. God of grace, your Son, Jesus, was born without wealth.*

People: *Forgive us when we are selfish or ignore the poor.*

Leader: *The shepherds left their sheep to go to Bethlehem.*

People: *Forgive us when we don't listen to your call.*

Leader: *For all the sins we have done*

People: *and for all the good we have failed to do.*

All: *Forgive and heal us. Amen.*

Prayers

Wonderful Counselor, send your angels to watch over us.
Mighty God, drive away fears or worries that keep us awake.
Prince of Peace, speak to us in our dreams.
Immanuel, give us faith that you are always with us.

The Lord's Prayer

Closing

Guide us waking, O God, and guard us sleeping;
that awake we may watch with Christ,
and asleep we may rest in peace.
Amen.

Epiphany – Morning

Opening

Leader: *God's glory shines among us.*
People: *Let us gather in stillness and silence.*

Holy silence or lighting of a candle or incense

Leader: *God, open our lips,*
People: *and our mouth shall proclaim your praise.*
All: *Glory to the Triune God—who is Love, who is Truth, and who is Wisdom (†)—as it was in the beginning, is now, and ever shall be. World without end. Alleluia.*

Leader: *Let us pray:*
All: *God of grace,*
you open our hearts, know our hopes,
and see our true selves.
Let your Holy Spirit inspire us
to perfectly love you
and to love our neighbors as ourselves.
In Jesus' name we pray.
Amen.

Scripture

Jesus came from Galilee to the Jordan River to be baptized by his cousin John. But John tried to stop him, saying, "I need to be baptized by you. Why do you come to me?" Jesus replied, "Let it be so now; it is fitting for us to do this to fulfill all justice." Then John agreed. As soon as Jesus was baptized, he went up out of the water. At that moment heaven was opened, and he saw the Spirit of God descending like a

dove and alighting on him. And a voice from heaven said,
"This is my Son, whom I love; with him I am well pleased."
—Matthew 3:13-17 (adapted)

Invitation

The way that God looks at Jesus at his baptism reveals the way that God looks at you every moment of your life—you are a child of God who is loved forever. This is true of everyone who has ever lived. During this season, pray each day that Christ will teach you to see that each person is a child of God who deserves love and justice.

Prayers

Let us pray:
God of the magi, open our hearts to the wisdom of different lands.
God of baptism, help us to die to sin and rise with your Son.
God who shines on mountains, let us hear your voice in nature.
God of feasts, may all who have died join us at the Eucharist.
For what else shall we pray?

Lord's Prayer

Closing

Leader: *God's glory shines among us.*
People: *Thanks be to God.*

Epiphany – Evening

Opening

Leader: *Pour out the Holy Spirit's light*
People: *on all we think or dream tonight.*
Leader: *Light and peace, in Jesus Christ our Savior.*
People: *Thanks be to God.*

Epiphany Collect

God of surprises,
you led the magi from the East
to find your Son, Jesus;
you led Jesus to the river
to join our deepest needs in baptism;
you led Jesus to a wedding
to show God's overflowing joy;
you led Jesus up a mountain
where his face shone like the sun.
Help us to find you shining
where we don't expect to see you.
Reveal your love at work
in all people, places, and things.
Amen.

Scripture

Jesus took three disciples—Peter, James and John—and led them up a high mountain by themselves. There he was transfigured before them. His face shone like the sun, and his clothes became as white as the light. Just then there appeared before them Moses and Elijah, talking with Jesus. Peter offered to build them tents and while he was still speaking, a bright cloud covered them, and a voice from the cloud said, "This is my Son, whom I love; with him I am well pleased. Listen to Jesus!" Matthew 17:1-5 (adapted)

Reflecting on the Day

- *Who or what are you grateful for today?*
- *Think about your day. What activities did you do? What feelings did you have? What did you notice?*
- *Looking back at your day, did God show up somewhere you weren't expecting?*

Confession

Leader: *In the gentle light of Christ, let us confess our sins. God of grace, the Holy Family welcomed magi traveling from afar.*

People: *Forgive us when we fail to welcome people who are different from us.*

Leader: *Mary, at the wedding, expected Jesus to turn water into wine.*

People: *Forgive us when we lose faith that Jesus will act in our lives.*

Leader: *For all the sins we have done*

People: *and for all the good we have failed to do.*

All: *Forgive and heal us. Amen.*

Prayers

God of dreams, send your angels to watch over us.
Shining Son, drive away fears or worries that keep us awake.
Christ our guide, lead us to your love.
God of our ancestors, give us faith in life after death.

The Lord's Prayer

Closing

Guide us waking, O God, and guard us sleeping,
that awake we may watch with Christ,
and asleep we may rest in peace.
Amen.

Lent – Morning

Opening

Leader: *Search me, O God, and know my heart.*
People: *Let us gather in stillness and silence.*

Holy silence or lighting of a candle or incense

Leader: *Jesus said, "You shall love the Lord your God with all your heart, all your soul, and all your mind. This is the first and greatest commandment."*
People: *"And the second is like it: love your neighbor as yourself."*

Leader: *Let us confess our sins against God and our neighbor.*
All: *Loving God, we are sorry*
for the hurtful things we have thought, said, or done,
and for not doing the things we should have done.
We ask for your forgiveness.
Set us on your way
and make us whole.
Amen.

Scripture

After Jesus' baptism, the Spirit immediately drove him out into the wilderness. He was in the wilderness for forty days, tempted by Satan. He was among the wild animals, and the angels took care of him. After his cousin John was arrested, Jesus came into Galilee announcing God's good news, saying, "The time is fulfilled, and the kingdom of God is at hand. Change your hearts and lives, and trust this good news." — Mark 1:12-14 (adapted)

Invitation

Over the forty days of Lent, pray each day by imagining yourself in the wilderness. Imagine Jesus at your side with the Holy Spirit quietly guiding you. Prepare to hear God's voice, find forgiveness, overcome temptations, be visited by angels, and discover the kingdom of God growing within you and around you.

Prayers

In this wilderness season, let us pray:
God of Abraham and Sarah, even with our faults, bless us so that we may bless others.
God of Moses and Miriam, help us to stand for justice and freedom.
God of John the Baptist, guide us to turn our lives towards your love.
God of Jesus, give us faith that the dead shall be raised.
For what else shall we pray?

Lord's Prayer

Closing

Leader: *Search me, O God, and know my heart.*
People: *Thanks be to God.*

Lent – Evening

Opening

Leader: *The Lord makes the wilderness like Eden,*
People: *the desert like the garden of God's kingdom.*
Leader: *Light and peace, in Jesus Christ our Savior.*
People: *Thanks be to God.*

Lent Collect

God of mercy and forgiveness,
you made us to love you and your creation,
and to love our neighbors as ourselves,
but we stray from you and fall into sin
when we choose to do hurtful things.
Guide us through the forty days of Lent,
to come closer to you with prayer, fasting, and giving.
In Jesus' name we pray.
Amen.

Scripture - *The Beatitudes*

From a mountain, Jesus taught the crowds: Blessed are the poor in spirit for the kingdom of heaven is theirs. Blessed are the sorrowful, for they shall find comfort. Blessed are the meek, for they shall inherit the earth. Blessed are those who hunger and thirst for justice, for they shall be satisfied. Blessed are the merciful, for they shall be shown mercy. Blessed are the pure in heart, for they shall see God. Blessed are the peacemakers, for they shall be God's children. Blessed are those who have suffered for doing what is right, for the kingdom of heaven is theirs. —Matthew 5:1-10 (NRSV adapted)

Reflecting on the Day

- *Who or what are you grateful for today?*
- *Think about your day. What activities did you do? What feelings did you have? What did you notice?*
- *As you imagine yourself in the wilderness with Jesus, does he have anything to tell you?*

Confession

Leader: *In the gentle light of Christ, let us confess our sins. God of grace, in the wilderness Jesus prepared for the kingdom of God.*

People: *Forgive us when we ignore the Spirit's guidance.*

Leader: *In the wilderness, the Israelites built a golden calf and worshiped it.*

People: *Forgive us when we worship wealth, idols, or anything other than you.*

Leader: *For all the sins we have done*

People: *and for all the good we have failed to do.*

All: *Forgive and heal us. Amen.*

Prayers

God of heaven, send your angels to watch over us.
Voice from the flame, drive away fears or worries that keep us awake.
Source of rainbows, give us hope in new beginnings.
Giver of promises, give us faith in life after death.

The Lord's Prayer

Closing

Guide us waking, O God, and guard us sleeping,
that awake we may watch with Christ,
and asleep we may rest in peace.
Amen.

Holy Week – Morning

Opening

Leader: *Jesus set his face to go to Jerusalem.*
People: *Let us gather in stillness and silence.*

Holy silence or lighting of a candle or incense

Leader: *For us, Christ became obedient unto death,*
People: *even death on a cross.*
All: *Holy God, Holy and Mighty, Holy Immortal One,*
have mercy upon us.

Leader: *Let us pray:*
All: *God of grace,*
you open our hearts, know our hopes,
and see our true selves.
Let your Holy Spirit inspire us
to perfectly love you
and to love our neighbors as ourselves.
In Jesus' name we pray.
Amen.

Scripture

On the night he was betrayed, the Lord Jesus took bread, and when he had given thanks, he broke it and said, "This is my body, which is for you; do this in memory of me." In the same way, after supper he took the cup, saying, "This cup is the new covenant in my blood; do this, whenever you drink it, in memory of me." For whenever you eat this bread and drink this cup, you proclaim the Lord's death until he comes.
—1 Corinthians 11:23-26, (NIV, adapted)

Invitation

During Holy Week, we walk with Jesus all the way to his death on the cross, and we carry his body to the tomb. Even in the worst moments of his life, God was always with Jesus. The same good news is true for all people: even in our worst moments God remains with us. Like the women who refused to leave as he was suffering, like the man who helped him carry his cross, ask yourself throughout the day, "How can I help someone who is hurting?"

Prayers

Let us pray:
God of friendship, let us treasure each meal with those we love.
God of forgiveness, guide us to love our enemies.
God of the cross, open our eyes and hearts to those in pain.
God of promise, give us confidence in your victory over death. (†)
For what else shall we pray?

The Lord's Prayer

Closing

Leader: *Jesus set his face to go to Jerusalem.*
People: *Thanks be to God.*

Holy Week – Evening

Opening

Leader: *This is how everyone will know that you are my disciples,*

People: *when you love each other.*

Leader: *Light and peace, in Jesus Christ our Lord.*

People: *Thanks be to God.*

Holy Week Collect

God who faces and conquers death,
As you entered Jerusalem on a donkey,
let us be humble and allow our lives to follow your plan.
As you cleansed the temple,
replace our greed with prayer.
As you washed your disciples' feet,
lead us to serve rather than be served.
As you descended to the dead,
give us faith that your love is with us even in death.
Amen.

Scripture

For I am convinced that neither death nor life, neither angels nor demons, neither the present nor the future, nor any powers, neither height nor depth, nor anything else in all creation, will be able to separate us from the love of God that is in Christ Jesus our Lord. —Romans 8:38-39

Reflecting on the Day

- *Who or what are you grateful for today?*
- *Think about your day. What activities did you do? What feelings did you have? What did you notice?*
- *Did you notice anyone who was afraid, hurting, or sad? How could you be their friend or do something friendly for them?*

Confession

Leader: *In the gentle light of Christ, let us confess our sins. God of grace, Saint Peter denied his friendship with Jesus three times.*

People: *Forgive us when we don't act like we are friends with you.*

Leader: *Simon of Cyrene helped Jesus carry the cross.*

People: *Forgive us when we fail to help others in need.*

Leader: *For all the sins we have done*

People: *and for all the good we have failed to do.*

All: *Forgive and heal us. Amen.*

Prayers

God of friendship, watch over us in our sleep tonight.
God of forgiveness, cast away fears or guilt that keeps us awake.
God of the cross, comfort those who live in fear, pain, or suffering.
God of promise, let us face death confident in our eternal life in Christ.

The Lord's Prayer

Closing

Guide us waking, O God, and guard us sleeping,
that awake we may watch with Christ,
and asleep we may rest in peace.
Amen.

Easter – Morning

Opening

Leader: *We have been raised with Christ.*
People: *Let us gather in stillness and silence.*

Holy silence or lighting of a candle or incense

Leader: *God, open our lips.*
People: *And our mouth shall proclaim your praise.*
All: *Glory to the Triune God—who is Love, who is Truth, and who is Wisdom (†)—as it was in the beginning, is now, and ever shall be. World without end. Alleluia.*

Leader: *Let us pray:*
All: *God of grace,*
you open our hearts, know our hopes,
and see our true selves.
Let your Holy Spirit inspire us
to perfectly love you
and to love our neighbors as ourselves.
In Jesus' name we pray.
Amen.

Scripture

At the empty tomb, the angel said to the women, "Do not be afraid; I know that you are looking for Jesus, who was crucified. He is not here; for he has been raised, as he said. Come, see the place where he lay. Then go quickly and tell his disciples, 'He has been raised from the dead, and indeed he is going ahead of you to Galilee. There you will see him.' This is my message for you." —Matthew 28:5-7 (adapted)

Invitation

We have the Easter story because people had the courage to proclaim what others thought was impossible. They shared their stories of encountering the resurrected Jesus. Like Mary Magdalene after Jesus approached her in the garden, like the disciples after breaking bread with him on the road to Emmaus, or like the apostle Paul after meeting Jesus on the road to Damascus, throughout the fifty days of Easter, practice sharing how you've felt Jesus alive in your life.

Prayers

Let us pray:
God of miracles, give us faith that, like Jesus at Easter, our bodies will someday rise from the dead.
Risen Christ, reveal yourself in the meals we share.
Ascending Son, bring all creation into your heavenly kingdom.
Holy Spirit, fill our hearts to share your good news with all humankind. (†)
For what else shall we pray?

The Lord's Prayer

Closing

Leader: *We have been raised with Christ.*
People: *Thanks be to God.*

Easter – Evening

Opening

Leader: *Alleluiah, Christ is risen!*
People: *The Lord is risen, indeed. Alleluiah!*
Leader: *Light and peace, in Jesus Christ our Savior.*
People: *Thanks be to God.*

Easter Collect

God who overcame death with love:
As you approached Mary in the garden,
speak to us in the beauty of creation.
As you taught the disciples how to read scripture,
let the stories of the Bible set our hearts on fire.
As you showed your scars to doubting Thomas,
give us the eyes of faith to trust in your resurrection.
As you filled your followers with the Holy Spirit,
guide us to discover what gifts we have to share.
Amen.

Scripture

After Easter, Jesus appeared to his followers over a period of forty days and spoke about the kingdom of God. . . . The apostles asked him, "Lord, are you at this time going to restore the kingdom to Israel?" He said to them: "It is not for you to know the times or dates the Father has set by his own authority. But you will receive power when the Holy Spirit comes on you; and you will be my witnesses in Jerusalem, and in all Judea and Samaria, and to the ends of the earth." After he said this, he was taken up before their very eyes, and a cloud hid him from their sight.
—Acts 1:3,6-9 (adapted)

Reflecting on the Day

- *Who or what are you grateful for today?*
- *Think about your day. What activities did you do? What feelings did you have? What did you notice?*
- *Where did you sense Jesus alive in your life today? Was it through another person, something you did, or something you felt inside?*

General Thanksgiving

Living God, firstborn from the dead,
we give you thanks and praise,
for all the blessings of this life,
but above all for your eternal love
revealed through the resurrection of Jesus Christ.
And, we pray, fill us up with so much love,
that with truly thankful hearts we may share that love with others,
not only with our lips, but in our lives,
by giving up ourselves to your service,
and by walking beside you
in holiness and justice all our days;
through Jesus Christ our Savior,
to whom, with you and the Holy Spirit,
be honor and glory throughout all ages.
Amen.

Prayers

God the Father, watch over us in our sleep tonight.
God the Son, cast away fears or guilt that keep us awake.
God the Spirit, renew our hopes and dreams.
Resurrected Christ, draw all who have died into eternal life. (†)

The Lord's Prayer

Closing

Guide us waking, O God, and guard us sleeping;
that awake we may watch with Christ,
and asleep we may rest in peace.
Amen. Alleluia.

Season After Pentecost – Morning

Opening

Leader: *God's power, alive in us, does more than we can imagine.*
People: *Let us gather in stillness and silence.*

Pause for 10 seconds of holy silence or lighting of the candle

Leader: *God, open our lips,*
People: *and our mouth shall proclaim your praise.*
All: *Glory to the Father, and to the Son, and to the Holy Spirit: one God and Mother of us all, (†) as it was in the beginning, is now, and will be forever. Alleluia.*

Leader: *Let us pray:*
All: *God of grace,*
you open our hearts, know our hopes,
and see our true selves.
Let your Holy Spirit inspire us
to perfectly love you
and to love our neighbors as ourselves.
In Jesus' name we pray.
Amen.

Scripture

When the day of Pentecost came, Jesus' closest friends and mother, Mary, were all together in one place. Suddenly a sound like the blowing of a very strong wind came from heaven and filled the whole house where they were sitting. They saw what seemed to be tongues of fire that divided and

came to rest on each of them. All of them were filled with the Holy Spirit and began to speak in other languages as the Spirit empowered them. —Acts 2:1-4 (adapted)

Invitation

Green is the color used to show that it is the season after Pentecost. It is the growing season—when we grow into the Body of Christ. The Holy Spirit breathes the life of Christ into us and grows the flame of God's love in our hearts. Let us live the questions: "How am I growing closer to Jesus today?" and "What can I do to help someone else grow closer to God?"

Prayers

Let us pray:
Spirit of the living God, fall fresh on us like rain.
Spirit of truth, shine on us like the sun.
Spirit of creation, breathe your life into our lives.
Holy Comforter, ground us in the soil of the saints and souls who dwell with you in heaven. (†)
For what else shall we pray?

The Lord's Prayer

Closing

Leader: *God's power, alive in us, does more than we can ask for or imagine.*
People: *Thanks be to God.*

Season After Pentecost – Evening

Opening

Leader: *Those who live in love live in God,*
People: *and God lives in them.*
Leader: *Light and peace, in Jesus Christ our Lord.*
All: *Thanks be to God.*

Collect

Eternal God, you created us in your image,
and you plant holy seeds of love in each person.
Like your prophets, let us grow in wisdom and in speaking up for what's right.
Like the disciples, nurture us to hear your call and walk with Jesus.
Like the saints, let your love grow in us and shine through our lives.
May we bear fruit of the Spirit for the world;
through Jesus Christ our Savior.
Amen.

Scripture

Let us love one another, for love comes from God. Everyone who loves has been born of God and knows God. . . . God is love. This is how God showed his love among us: He sent his one and only Son into the world that we might live through him. . . . Dear friends, since God so loved us, we also ought to love one another. No one has ever seen God, but if we love one another, God lives in us and his love is made complete in us. This is how we know that we live in God and God in us: He has given us of his Spirit. —1 John 4:7-9, 11-13

Reflecting on the Day

- *Who or what are you grateful for today?*
- *Think about your day. What activities did you do? What feelings did you have? What did you notice?*
- *How did you grow closer to Jesus today? What did you do to try and help someone else grow closer to God's love?*

Confession

Leader: *In the gentle light of Christ, let us confess our sins.*

All: *Loving God, we are sorry*
for the hurtful things we have thought, said, or done,
And for not doing the things we should have done.
We ask for your forgiveness.
Set us on your way and make us whole.
Amen.

Prayers

Spirit of the living God, fall fresh on us as we sleep.
Spirit of truth, visit us in our visions and dreams.
Holy Spirit, dwell in us—Body of Christ.
Holy Comforter, may all who have died rest in your peace and rise in glory. (†)

The Lord's Prayer

Closing

Guide us waking, O God, and guard us sleeping,
that awake we may watch with Christ,
and asleep we may rest in peace.
Amen.

PART 2

Praying Through the Year

One of the most life-changing invitations I ever received came from a man named Saint Ignatius. (Not the Saint Ignatius of Antioch, who was slain by a fierce wild beast, but Saint Ignatius *of Loyola*—founder of the Society of Jesus in 1540.) A simple but revolutionary suggestion, Saint Ignatius invited his listeners to "find God in all things." At the core of this spiritual exercise is the belief that God is found not only in worship and in the Christian tradition, but God can be found in every person, place, and event. Put differently, God's loving presence flows through everything.

This section seeks to find God in all things related to the calendars that shape our lives. As a school chaplain, I live with one foot in the liturgical calendar celebrating holy feasts and saints, and the other foot in the secular calendar celebrating national holidays and matters related to diversity, equity, and inclusion.

My hope is that these prayers name how God can be found in occasions like Lunar New Year, Labor Day, Women's History Month, or Indigenous Peoples' Day, just as much as God can be found in occasions celebrating Saint Michael and All Angels, the Blessing of the Animals, or the Transfiguration of Our Lord Jesus Christ.

While all these prayers were originally used in a school setting, I have gone on to share many of them at church and with my family. No matter where it's used, I hope this section helps you find God in the stories and special occasions that we celebrate throughout the year. Each month of the year is a new invitation to find God at work in our lives.

January

New Year's Day / The Holy Name of Jesus (1/1)

Therefore, God highly honored Christ and gave Jesus a name above all names. —Philippians 2:9

Eternal God, whose Spirit fills time,
each January 1st we celebrate both New Year's Day
and the holy name of Jesus,
the Son of God and Savior of the world.
As we journey through another year,
let us remember that Jesus journeys with us
each year, each day, each hour, each moment.
May the love of Christ that's planted in every heart,
come to life and bear the fruit of the Spirit.
Amen.

The Rev. Dr. Martin Luther King, Jr. Day (1/15)

Let justice roll down like waters, and righteousness like an ever-flowing stream —Amos 5:24

God of peacemakers,
we celebrate the life of your prophet Martin Luther King, Jr.
Be with us now, Martin.
Pray beside us, pray for us, and pray with us.
Give us the vision to see each person as somebody loved by God;
bless us with strength to love our enemies and practice nonviolence;
and inspire us with your dream of a world overflowing with justice and freedom.
We ask all of this through Christ Jesus,
who, like Martin, gave his life for the sake of love.
Amen.

Florence Li Tim-Oi, Priest (1/24)

(On January 25, 1944, in Hong Kong, Florence was the first woman in modern history to be ordained a priest.)

God of courage, whose light shines through the saints,
we celebrate the life of Florence Li Tim-Oi.
Be with us now, Florence.
Pray beside us, pray for us, and pray with us.
Following the example of your life in China,
give us the vision to see God doing new things around the globe;
bless us with strength to remain faithful
if we are threatened, harmed, or in places torn by war;
and inspire us to do what others believe is impossible.
We ask all of this through Christ Jesus,
whose love shines through the saints.
Amen.

Holocaust Remembrance Day (1/27)

If only my head were a spring of water, and my eyes a fountain of tears, I would weep day and night for the wounds of my people. —Jeremiah 9:1

God who weeps,
this Holocaust Remembrance Day,
we remember the lives of the more than 6 million Jews
who were murdered in Europe between 1941 and 1945.
May we honor their lives with our promise
to keep their memory alive,
to understand the evil of anti-Semitism within our world,
to identify and reject all forms of discrimination and hatred,
and to respect and defend every human being.
Amen.

February

Black History Month

The Lord is the Spirit, and where the Lord's Spirit is, there is freedom. —2 Corinthians 3:17

Loving God, source of all diversity,
your Holy Spirit dwells in every tribe, race, and culture of the world.
As we celebrate Black History Month,
guide us to see you in Black love that grows,
in Black lives that matter, and Black dreams that shine.
Keep every Black person in your love and protection,
help us to tell Black history truthfully,
and guide our nation to celebrate Black history,
not just during this month but every month.
We pray this alongside Absalom Jones and all your Black saints.
Amen.

The Presentation of Our Lord Jesus Christ in the Temple (2/2)

Since the children share in flesh and blood, Jesus also shared the same things in the same way. —Hebrews 2:14

Gentle God, you love all children,
and you want them to grow in wisdom and truth.
As Mary and Joseph brought Jesus, your Son,
to be presented in the Temple,
inspire us to offer ourselves and families to you.
Cleanse our hearts and fill us with your Holy Spirit,
so that your love becomes our love,
your life becomes our life,
and our bodies become the Body of Christ.
We pray this in the name of Jesus,
who was once a child, and who remains with all children.
Amen.

Lunar New Year (the first new moon of a lunar calendar)

The moon and the stars to rule the night—God's faithful love lasts forever! —Psalm 136:9

God of the heavens, of moon, sun, and stars,
we give thanks for the Lunar New Year,
and for all the cultures of the earth that pause
to celebrate peace, family, and the goodness of life.
Bless us this year with health, wisdom, and wealth
so that we may share these freely with others,
and live together as one human family;
through him who is the beginning and the end,
your Son Jesus Christ our Lord.
Amen.

Saint Valentine's Day (2/14)

Love each other, because love is from God, and everyone who loves is born from God and knows God. 1 John 4:7

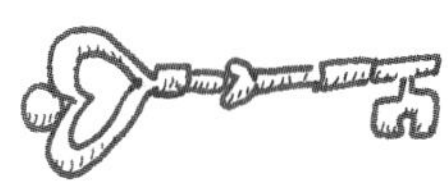

God of sacrificial love,
whose light shines through the saints,
we give thanks for Saint Valentine,
who gave his life for you and is alive with you in heaven.
Be with us now, Saint Valentine.
Pray beside us, pray for us, and pray with us.
Teach us to find God in the different forms of love—
in the love we find in romance,
in the love we share between friends,
in the love that bonds a family together,
and, most of all, in a love that lays down its life for others.
We ask all of this through Christ Jesus,
whose love shines through the saints.
Amen.

March

Women's History Month

Strength and honor are her clothing; she is confident about the future. —*Proverbs 31:25*

God of Sarah, Hagar, Rebekah, and Rachel,
you blessed us so that we may be a blessing to others,
celebrating the goodness and value of each person.
This Women's History Month,
we ask that you bless the lives of women throughout history,
bless the lives of women around the world,
bless the life of each woman present with us now,
and bless the future lives of women who will come after us.
Through your eternal love,
transform each of us and empower us
to work towards justice, recognition, and fullness of life
for women and girls everywhere.
Amen.

International Women's Day (3/8)

I can do all things through Christ who strengthens me. —
Philippians 4:13 (NRSV)

O Heavenly Mother,
in recognition of International Women's Day,
we pause to celebrate the lives and dignity
of women throughout history,
women around the world,
and each woman present with us now.
We raise our voices and demand respect, justice,
and fullness of life for all women—
especially women whose freedoms and safety are ignored.
Amen.

Saint Patrick's Day (3/17)

Go and make disciples of all nations, baptizing them in the name of the Father and of the Son and of the Holy Spirit.
—Matthew 28:19

God of forgiveness, whose light shines through the saints,
we give thanks for the life and love of Saint Patrick of Ireland,
who died on this day and is alive with you in heaven.
Be with us now, Saint Patrick.
Pray beside us, pray for us, and pray with us.
Teach us to trust that Christ is always within us and around us;
guide us to befriend people from different nations;
and inspire us to see God's love reflected in the natural world.
We ask all of this in the strong Name of the Trinity,
the Three in One, and One in Three.
Amen.

The Annunciation of Our Lord Jesus Christ to the Blessed Virgin Mary (3/25 – nine months before Christmas)

> *Therefore, the Lord will give you a sign. The young woman is pregnant and is about to give birth to a son, and she will name him Immanuel. —Isaiah 7:14*

God of good news,
you sent the angel Gabriel to Mary,
to announce the message that she had been chosen
to be the mother of God
by giving birth to Jesus, the Son.
Like Mary, fill us with your grace,
make us aware of your angels,
and shine your holy light
on the desire deep within all souls
to let your love be grown in us.
Amen.

April

National Poetry Month

In the beginning was the Word, and the Word was with God and the Word was God. —John 1:1

Eternal Word, Creator of all things,
this National Poetry Month, as we celebrate the power of words,
we remember that through your Word
you spoke the universe into being, created life,
and blessed humans with the gift of speech.
Plant your Holy Spirit within our souls,
that we may create poetry that praises you,
that expresses ourselves, that shares wisdom,
and that bears the fruit of faith, hope, and love.
We pray this in the name Jesus, the Word made flesh.
Amen.

Arab-American History Month

Abraham looked up and saw three men standing nearby. So he quickly left the entrance to his tent to greet them. He bowed low to the ground. —Genesis 18:2

Loving God, source of all diversity,
your Holy Spirit dwells in every tribe, race, and culture of the world,
this month we celebrate your children who are Arab Americans.
Keep all Arab Americans in your love and protection,
fill the world with respect and hospitality,
inspire our churches and schools with the rich religious
traditions of the Arab and Middle Eastern world,
and guide us, as a nation, to celebrate Arab cultures
and defend Arab peoples' rights

not just during this month but every month.
Amen.

Earth Day (April 22)

The earth is the Lord's, and everything in it, the world, and all who live in it. Psalm 24:1 (NIV)

Creator of our beautiful and fragile planet,
on this Earth Day we celebrate our common home.
We give thanks for the wonders of the sea, sky, and land.
We praise you for the miracle of life
and for the diversity of life forms—
from bacteria and bugs to blue whales and babies.
We remember the creation belongs to you alone,
and we affirm the great responsibility you have given us:
to care for creation and protect life on Earth.
For your sake, and for the sake for the future,
may we grow in our love for the Earth and all life;
through Jesus Christ our Savior.
Amen.

Saint Mark the Evangelist (April 25)

Jesus said to the apostles, "Go into the whole world and proclaim the good news to every creature. —Mark 16:15

God of good news, whose light shines through the saints,
we give thanks for the life and writing of Saint Mark,
author of the Bible's earliest gospel of Jesus Christ.
Be with us now, Saint Mark.
Pray beside us, pray for us, and pray with us.
Guide us to share God's love with simplicity and urgency;
help us to understand that following Jesus can challenging;
and, even if we can't see it,
give us the confidence to believe in the resurrection.
We ask all of this through Christ Jesus,
whose love shines through the saints.
Amen.

May

Asian American and Pacific Islander (AAPI) Heritage Month

When the Spirit of Truth comes, he will guide you in all truth. —John 16:13

Loving God, sourcc of all diversity,
your Holy Spirit dwells in every tribe, race, and culture of the world,
This month we celebrate your children who are Asian Americans or Pacific Islanders.
Keep every Asian American and Pacific Islander in your love and protection,
inspire our churches and schools with the rich religious traditions of Asia and the Pacific Islands,
and guide us, as a nation, to learn from the past
and celebrate AAPI cultures and accomplishments,
not just during this month but every month.
Amen.

Mental Health Awareness

Come to me, all you who are struggling hard and carrying heavy loads, and I will give you rest. —Matthew 11:28

God of mindfulness,
knowing that May is Mental Health Awareness Month,
we pray for everyone struggling with mental health problems
—especially those who are depressed, anxious, or heartbroken.
Be with those whose voices go unheard,
whose health is ignored,
or whose rights are not recognized or respected.
In difficult times and our darkest hours,
give us the confidence that you are with us, O God,
and that the promise of peace will someday be fulfilled.
Amen.

Mother's Day

The angel came to Mary and said, "Rejoice, favored one! The Lord is with you!" —Luke 1:28

God of all creation,
bless all mothers and mother figures
whom you have called to care for your children.
Help moms everywhere to grow deeper in the Spirit;
like Moses' mother, Jochebed, give them determination and faith;
like Mary, Jesus' mother, give them grace and confidence;
like Saint Monica, give them the heart to always pray for their children.
May the love of our mothers here on earth
lead us to the everlasting love of you,
our Heavenly Mother.
Amen.

Memorial Day (last Monday of May)

Comfort, comfort my people! says your God. —Isaiah 40:1

O Judge of the nations,
with grateful hearts
we remember the men and women of our country
who gave their lives trying to secure freedom for others.
Grant that we may not rest
until all the people of this world share in true freedom
and accept its responsibilities.
Amen.

June

Pride Month Prayer (see also National Coming Out Day in October)

You knit me together while I was still in my mother's womb.
I give thanks to you that I was marvelously set apart.
—Psalm 139:13-14

God of rainbows and surprises,
of David and Jonathan,
of Saint Joan of Arc and Pauli Murray,
of the beloved disciple and all humanity,
you are the source of all true love.
This month we celebrate the members of our world
who are proud of the love you have poured into their hearts
and who are true to what your Spirit has spoken in their souls.
We bless the many ways of being human and loving others,
and we commit ourselves to making wherever we go
a place where each LGBTQ person is welcomed, honored, and loved.
In Jesus' name we pray.
Amen.

Father's Day

While still a long way off, the father saw his child and was moved with compassion. The father ran to the child, and hugged and kissed the child. —Luke 15:20, adapted

Tender God, you hold us in your everlasting arms.
Bless all fathers and father figures
whom you have called to care for your children.
Help dads everywhere to grow deeper in the Spirit;
like Joseph, give them the strength to love and to listen;
like David, give them the wisdom to know and share their emotions;
like Saint Francis, give them the gentleness and peace of Christ.
May the love of our fathers here on earth
lead us to the everlasting love of you,
our Heavenly Father.
Amen.

Juneteenth (June 19)

Jesus read: "The Spirit of the Lord...has sent me to proclaim freedom for the prisoners...to set the oppressed free, to proclaim the year of the Lord's favor." —Luke 4:18-19 (ESV)

God of justice, who hears the cries of captives
and commands all people to work for their neighbors' freedom,
today we remember June 19th in 1865:
the day when the delayed news of slavery's end
finally reached the last corner of America.
We remember the progress our country has made
in the march to win freedom for all,
but we are mindful that this march is incomplete,
that we still have much work to do.
Forgive our country for the sins of slavery,
empower us to repay the wrongs that have been done,
and, with Christ by our side, let us march on till victory is won.
Amen.

World Refugee Day (June 20)

An angel from the Lord appeared to Joseph in a dream and said, "Get up. Take the child and his mother and escape to Egypt." —Matthew 2:13

God of all the nations,
your love has no borders,
and you invite all people into your kingdom;
this World Refugee Day, and every day,
teach us to hear the cries of refugees and immigrants,
guide us to see them with your eyes of compassion,
help us to welcome them with words of hope,
and open our hearts so that we may open our arms
and care for our neighbors from other countries,
just as strangers cared for Jesus and his family when they were refugees.
In Jesus' name we pray.
Amen.

John the Baptist (June 24)

You, child, will be called a prophet of the Most High, for you will go before the Lord to prepare his way. —Luke 1:76

God of the wilderness and water,
whose Holy Spirit calls us to new life,
we give thanks for the birth, life, and call of John the Baptist,
and we remember the promises of baptism:
to reject evil and ask for forgiveness,
to seek and serve Christ in all people,
to strive for justice, peace, and the common good,
and, most of all, to follow Jesus as our Savior.
May our words and deeds welcome others
into the baptized life of Christ.
Amen.

July

Pauli Murray (July 1)

There is no longer Jew or Greek, there is no longer slave or free, there is no longer male and female; for all of you are one in Christ Jesus. —Galatians 3:28

God of freedom, whose light shines through the saints,
we give thanks for the courageous life of Pauli Murray,
who died on this day and is alive with you in heaven.
Be with us now, Pauli.
Pray beside us, pray for us, and pray with us.
May your example free us from the chains of prejudice
and deliver us from fear of what we don't understand;
guide us to use our gifts for justice;
and let us sing of God's hope when our throats are weary.
We ask all of this through Christ Jesus,
whose love shines through the saints.
Amen.

Independence Day (July 4)

You were called to freedom, brothers and sisters; only don't let this freedom be an opportunity to feed your selfish desires, but serve each other through love. —Galatians 5:13

God of all nations,
we thank you for the dream of freedom that gave birth to America,
and we celebrate our values of democracy, equality, and self-governance.
Forgive us for the ways our country has failed
to live up to its dream and our values;
give us the humility to learn from other nations;
bless everyone who has sacrificed for the freedom of others;
and grant us Americans the wisdom to use our freedoms
to form a more perfect union,
establishing liberty and justice for all.
Amen.

Activists for Women's Rights (July 20)

She surveys a field and acquires it; from her own resources, she plants a vineyard. She works energetically; her arms are powerful. —Proverbs 31:16-17

God of justice, our heavenly Mother,
whose Spirit guides us into all truth and makes us free,
we celebrate everyone who has worked for girls' and women's rights—
Sojourner Truth, Elizabeth Cady Stanton, Pauli Murray, Malala Yousafzai, and countless others
who have stood against forces of injustice.
Let their examples and dreams inspire us
to work towards the just and fair treatment of women.
We pray this in the name of Christ Jesus,
through whom we are all children of God.
Amen.

Saint Mary Magdalene (July 22)

Mary Magdalene left and announced to the disciples, "I've seen the Lord." Then she told them what he said to her.
—John 20:18,

God of friendship, whose light shines through the saints,
we give thanks for the life and witness of Saint Mary Magdalene,
who was the first to approach Jesus' empty tomb
and encounter the living Christ on Easter morning.
Be with us now, Saint Mary Magdalene.
Pray beside us, pray for us, and pray with us.
Following your example, free us from pride
so we may ask God to cast away our inner demons;
guide us to always seek a deeper friendship with Christ;
and inspire us to be transformed by Jesus's resurrection.
We ask all of this through Christ Jesus,
whose love shines through the saints.
Amen.

August

The Transfiguration of Our Lord Jesus Christ (August 6)

Jesus took Peter, John, and James, and went up on a mountain to pray. As he was praying, the appearance of his face changed and his clothes flashed white like lightning.
—Luke 9:28-29

Eternal God,
who unites the past, present, and future,
as Jesus prayed on the mountain top,
help us to listen to your Spirit in nature;
as Jesus spoke with the prophets Moses and Elijah,
help the past to come alive in our prayers;
as Jesus brought close friends with him to pray,
help us to invite others into your presence;
as Jesus revealed the glory of his life after Easter,
help us to trust and the promise of resurrection;
through Jesus Christ our Savior.
Amen.

Clare of Assisi (August 11)

"The Spirit of the Lord is on me, because he has anointed me to proclaim good news to the poor." —Luke 4: 18

God of friendship, whose light shines through the saints,
we give thanks for the life and love of Saint Clare,
who died on this day and is alive with you in heaven.
Be with us now, Saint Clare.
Pray beside us, pray for us, and pray with us.
Free us from greed so we may befriend the poor as you did;
guide us to make friends with those who are misunderstood or rejected;
and inspire us to form communities of trust, devoted to prayer and service.
We ask all of this through Christ Jesus,
whose love shines through the saints.
Amen.

Saint Mary the Virgin, Mother of Our Savior Jesus Christ (August 15)

Mary said: From now on all generations will call me blessed, for the Mighty One has done great things for me—holy is his name. —Luke 1: 48-49

God of miracles, who makes all things possible,
we praise you for Mary,
the Mother of our Savior Jesus Christ,
who heard your holy call and said yes.
Help us to follow her in saying yes to you,
making a place for your love and justice
where others believe it is impossible.
Hail Mary, full of grace,
pray beside us, pray for us, and pray with us,
now and at the hour of our death.
Amen.

Senior Citizens Day (August 21)

If any of you are sick, they should call for the elders of the church, and the elders should pray over them, anointing them with oil in the name of the Lord. —James 5:14

God of our elders,
this Senior Citizens Day we pause to celebrate
the older adults in our lives and seniors throughout the world;
help us to seize our chances to spend time with them;
guide us to listen to their wisdom
and to learn from their victories and mistakes;
most of all, inspire us to carry on their love.
Amen.

September

Labor Day (first Monday in September)

"Come to me, all who labor and are heavy laden,
and I will give you rest." —Matthew 11:28

God of work and of rest,
who came to us as Jesus Christ the worker and craftsman,
we give thanks for all who labor
and we see that our lives rely on the work of others.
Guide us in the work we do,
that it fulfills our own needs and serves the common good;
make us mindful of the rights of workers, that they be treated fairly;
and fill us with concern for those who are out of work,
that we treat them with compassion and generosity.
We pray this in the name of Jesus,
who promised rest for all who labor.
Amen.

Holy Cross Day (September 14)

But as for me, God forbid that I should boast about anything
except for the cross of our Lord Jesus Christ. —Galatians 6:14

Living God, through Christ Jesus you suffered death on a cross.
By your holy cross, teach us that those who suffer are embraced by you instead of rejected.
Teach us to bear one another's suffering instead of ignoring it.
Teach to forgive our enemies and to break the cycle of violence.
Teach us to stand for what is right and true, even when threatened.
By your holy cross, give us faith that nothing—not even death—
can separate us from your love and the promise of resurrection.
We ask these things in the name of Jesus, the crucified one.
Amen.

Saint Matthew, Apostle and Evangelist (September 21)

Jesus saw a man named Matthew sitting and collecting taxes. He said to him, "Follow me," and he got up and followed him. —Matthew 9:9, adapted

God of good news, whose light shines through the saints,
we give thanks for the life and witness of Saint Matthew,
the tax collector who became your apostle and evangelist.
Be with us now, Saint Matthew.
Pray beside us, pray for us, and pray with us.
Following your example, may your Holy Spirit
free us from all greed and the selfish love of money;
guide us to always follow in the steps of Jesus;
and inspire us to share the good news of God's love.
We ask all of this through Christ Jesus,
whose love shines through the saints.
Amen.

Saint Michael and All Angels (September 29)

Jesus then added, "Very truly I tell you, you will see heaven open, and the angels of God ascending and descending on the Son of Man." —John 1:51, NIV

Eternal God, maker of heaven and earth,
we give thanks for Saint Michael and all the angels,
those heavenly guardians and messengers who forever sing your praise.
Be with us now, Saint Michael and every angel.
Pray beside us, pray for us, and pray with us.
Teach us to be guardians to one another,
especially the weak, the poor, and the needy;
guide us to be messengers of God's love and justice;
and inspire us to lift our hearts in praise
and see the world through heaven's eyes;
through Jesus Christ our Savior.
Amen.

October

Blessing of the Animals on the Feast of Saint Francis (October 4)

The righteous care for the needs of their animals.
—Proverbs 12:10

Blessed are you, Giver of Life, who makes all things good.
You called forth life that filled the sea, land, and sky.
You inspired Saint Francis to call all creatures his brothers and sisters.
We ask you to bless all of earth's creatures.
And we especially ask you to bless our pets.
Empower them to be good dogs, cuddly cats, and loyal companions.
Finally, give us a reverence for all living things and the beauty of creation.
Blessed are you, Lord our God, in all creatures great and small!
Amen.

Hispanic Heritage (September 15 to October 15)

May the Lord our God be with us, just as he was with our ancestors. May he never leave us or abandon us. —1 Kings 8:57

Loving God, source of all diversity,
your Holy Spirit dwells in every tribe, race, and culture of the world,
and we celebrate everyone with Hispanic heritage
—the descendants of Spain, Mexico,
the Caribbean, and Central and South America.
Keep every person with Hispanic heritage in your love and protection,
help all of us to join the call for liberation and justice,
and guide us, as a nation, to celebrate Hispanic cultures and rich spiritual traditions,
not just during this month but every month.
We pray this alongside Our Lady of Guadalupe, Oscar Romero,
and all your Hispanic saints.
Amen.

Indigenous Peoples' Day (second Monday in October)

Let all the rivers clap their hands; let the mountains rejoice out loud before the Lord because he is coming to establish justice on the earth! —Psalm 98:8-9

O God, Creator and Mother of all,
we celebrate all native American and indigenous people,
and with Christ we mourn the brutal conquest by the Europeans.
May God the Father fill us with love
so we may commit ourselves to truth-telling, justice, and healing.
May God the Son open America's hearts and minds
to the pain and broken promises that have been suffered,
and to the hopes and dreams that have survived;
and may God the Holy Spirit help America to repent
of the evil and sin committed by its ancestors,
and lead us into a new age of reconciliation.
Amen.

National Coming Out Day (October 11) (also see Pride Month Prayer)

Jesus shouted with a loud voice, "Lazarus, come out!"
—John 11:43

God of rainbows, source of truth and freedom,
we especially give thanks for National Coming Out Day,
which takes place each October 11th,
and we celebrate each brave gay, lesbian, bisexual, or trans person
who comes out to themselves, their families, and their friends;
and we pray for those who want to come out but have not
—especially those without a safe space to be themselves.
We affirm that diversity is divine,
that each LGBT person is a holy gift,
and that coming out is an expression of God's truth and love.
Amen.

November

Native American Heritage (see also Indigenous Peoples' Day in October)

Truth springs up from the ground; righteousness gazes down from heaven. —Psalm 85:11

Loving God, source of all diversity,
your Holy Spirit dwells in every tribe, race, and culture of the world,
and we celebrate everyone with Native American heritage
—the first peoples of North and South America.
Keep every person with this heritage in your love and protection;
bless them now and for generations to come;
and guide us, as a nation, to celebrate Native American cultures,
rights, and rich spiritual traditions,
not just during this month but every month.
We pray this alongside Saint Juan Diego, Saint O-kuh-ha-tah, and all
your Native American saints.
Amen.

Día de los Muertos (November 1 and 2)

God will wipe away every tear from their eyes. Death will be no more. —Revelation 21:4

God of all saints and all souls,
you welcome those who have died to rest with you in heaven,
and your love creates a bridge between the living and the dead;
wc givc thanks for thc Day of the Dead—Día de los Muertos—
when we remember our loved ones who have died;
through your love, help us to feel their presence;
help us to trust that Jesus is guiding them through the afterlife,
and give us faith that, someday,
we will all be reunited in our resurrected bodies;
through Jesus Christ our Savior.
Amen.

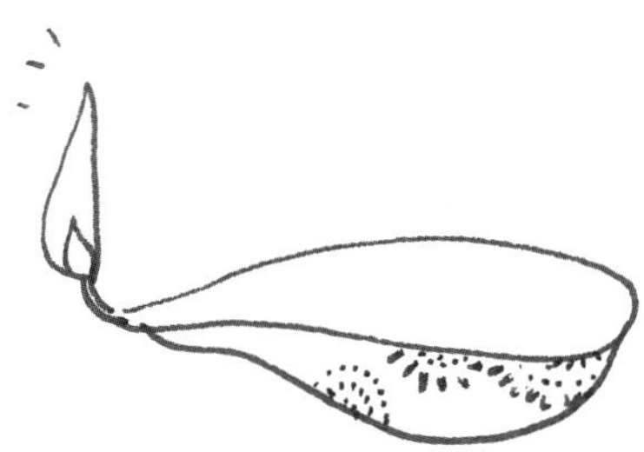

Veterans' Day (November 11)

Hate evil, love good, and establish justice at the city gate.
—Amos 5:15

God of all the nations,
this Veterans' Day we give thanks
for the men and women who served in the military
out of a sense of love for their neighbors,
out of the desire to protect the innocent,
and out of a responsibility to secure our freedoms.
Bless the veterans and their families;
heal all veterans wounded in body, mind, or spirit;
and help us to honor their service with our words and actions.
Amen.

Thanksgiving Day

Every good gift, every perfect gift, comes from above.
—James 1:17

God our Host,
as Jesus invites us to his table
to share in the life of God,
let us also invite you to our table this Thanksgiving Day.
Help us to tell our history with honesty, forgive us our trespasses,
and renew us with the gratitude of Christ:
grateful for the food, the table, and the people gathered round it;
grateful for the carpenter who shaped the wood;
grateful for the forest where the wood came from;
grateful for the rain and soil that allowed the trees to grow;
grateful for the earth in its orbit that provided seasons and sunlight;
grateful for the universe where countless suns and stars are shining.
We pray this in the name of Christ Jesus, the Son of God.
Amen.

December

World AIDS Day (12/1)

I was sick and you took care of me. —Matthew 25:36

God of care and healing,
as Jesus took care of those who were ill and excluded,
you call us to also care for and comfort the sick.
Today we especially pray for everyone living with HIV and AIDS.
Help us to follow your way of love
and provide health and care to all who have AIDS;
inspire us to speak out when people with AIDS are mistreated,
and give us creativity to learn new ways of prevention and healing.
May we always remember: when we care for the sick, we care for Christ.
Amen.

International Day of Persons with Disabilities (12/3)

The parts of the body that people think are the weakest are
the most necessary. —1 Corinthians 12:22

Loving God,
you are alive in each person,
on this International Day of Persons with Disabilities,
we ask that you open our hearts to see each disabled person
as a child of God who deserves respect, rights, and love;
inspire our minds to see the blessings that disabled persons offer
and to celebrate the gifts they possess;
empower us to speak up whenever a disabled person is disrespected;
and guide our hands to build your kingdom
where all are welcomed and treated fairly.
Amen.

Saint Nicholas' Day (12/6)

Jesus said, "I assure you that whoever doesn't welcome God's kingdom like a child will never enter it." Then he hugged the children and blessed them. —Mark 10:15-16

Gentle God, whose light shines through the saints,
we give thanks for the life of Saint Nicholas,
who died on this day and is alive with you in heaven.
Be with us now, Saint Nicholas.
Pray beside us, pray for us, and pray with us.
Teach us to care for, protect, and love each child;
inspire us to give generously to the poor;
and guide us to make the Christmas season a time
of compassion and not consumption.
We ask all of this through Christ Jesus,
whose love shines through the saints.
Amen.

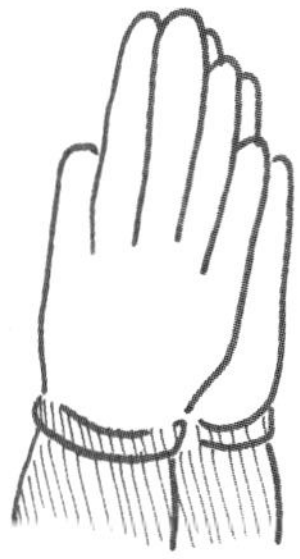

Saint Lucy's Day (12/13)

Let your face shine on your servant; save me in your unfailing love. —Psalm 31:16

God of courage, whose light shines through the saints,
we give thanks for the life of Saint Lucy,
who died on this day and is alive with you in heaven.
Be with us now, Saint Lucy.
Pray beside us, pray for us, and pray with us.
Teach us to see the world through your loving eyes;
give us courage to stand up for what is right;
and crown us with light to be a source of hope in times of darkness.
We ask all of this through Christ Jesus,
whose love shines through the saints.
Amen.

Café
BOOKS
Sale!
20%
BUS

PART 3

Praying through the Growing Season

When instructing children about prayer, I engage them in the following imaginative exercise.

Imagine you are a circle. This circle represents everything you are—your body, soul, and all the things that make you unique. When we pray for ourselves—whether praying for calm, for freedom, or for help falling asleep—we are asking God to be our partner in life. God wants to grow with us and is always waiting for us to ask for help.

Next, around the circle of yourself, imagine a ring. This ring represents the circle of friends and family that surround you. When we pray for family and friends, we root these relationships in God's love so that they grow deeper in goodness, truth, and beauty.

Around your circle of family and friends are more rings that include libraries, playgrounds, schools, coaches, first responders, and other places and people that make up the wider community. The final sections of this part of the book take places and people in our common life and bring them before God. Through prayer, our relationships with these places and people will grow in gratitude and value.

The more you pray, the more you will realize that God is at the center of your circle and every circle. Realizing this, it becomes easier to draw the circle of prayer wider and wider—so that prayer eventually encompasses all creation.

For Myself

For Goodness

God of grace, light of the world,
in the beginning you looked at everything you had made
and said that it was very good.
Be part of my vision, O God.
Look out through my eyes at the world you have made,
to see the goodness within me and surrounding me.
That I may see all things shining,
held together in your love;
through Jesus Christ our Savior.
Amen.

For Calm

God of peace,
as Jesus once commanded the storm to be still,
please speak now to the storms within me;
help calm my feelings and thoughts;
relax my body and center my soul;
send your Holy Spirit to lead me
in taking long, soft, and deep breaths;
and bless me with the faith that Christ is here with me,
and that the ocean within me is calm.
Amen.

For Compassion

God of mercy,
as Jesus looked at others with compassion,
and was moved to show them love,
please open the eyes of my heart,
that I might watch with Christ
and see others through heaven's eyes,

not ignoring their sadness, sickness, pain, or suffering,
but having compassion, showing kindness, and keeping the faith
that each person is a child of God and is worthy of love;
through Jesus Christ our Savior.
Amen.

Asking for Forgiveness

Gentle God, you want us to be free from guilt.
When it's hard for me to say "I'm sorry" and ask for forgiveness,
soften my heart and tear down my wall of shame.
Help me to know that, deep down,
forgiveness is freedom;
give me the trust that I will be forgiven;
and when I make mistakes or do what's wrong,
give me faith that deep down I am good and still worthy of love;
through Jesus Christ our Savior.
Amen.

For Rest

God of the sabbath,
when the work of creation was finished, you rested;
and you commanded us to pause, pray,
and celebrate the blessing of being alive.
Free us from our busy ways of life
and help us to make time to rest—
to rest in the beauty of the world,
to rest in the company of family and friends,
and to rest, O God, in your holy love.
Give us faith that Christ rests within our hearts.
In Jesus' name we pray.
Amen.

For Falling Asleep

Gentle God,
whose blessings outnumber the stars in our universe,
you gave us the gift of sleep,
where our minds, bodies, and souls are renewed.
Please drive away fears or worries that may keep me awake;
send your angels to keep me safe in my sleep;
speak to me in my dreams;
and please give me the light of Christ
to guide me when I wake.
In Jesus' name we pray.
Amen.

For Freedom from Greed

God of freedom,
you created us to share life with others,
and you blessed us so that we can be a blessing to all people.
Free us from every form of greed;
teach us to take no more than we need;
and guide us to define our lives, not by what we have,
but by the love and generosity of Christ.
In Jesus' name we pray.
Amen.

For Freedom from Fear

God of freedom,
you taught that perfect love removes all fear;
help me to trust that I am never alone;
that Jesus, the Good Shepherd, is always with me;
and that, with the perfect love of the Holy Spirit,
I can face my fears and conquer them through faith.
Amen.

For Freedom to Be Myself

God of freedom,
We are true to ourselves
when we are true to the love you have placed within us.
Bless me with the courage to be myself,
to be one with the breath of life,
to be free from hurtful judgments,
and to celebrate myself, and every person, as a child of God.
We pray this in the name of Jesus,
who told us that the truth will set us free.
Amen.

For My Family and Friends

Expecting a New Baby

God of grace,
when Mary and Elizabeth were pregnant
with Jesus and John the Baptist,
they rejoiced together for the miracle of life.
Like them, we give you thanks and praise
for the baby we are expecting.
Be with the mother and fetus,
keeping them safe and healthy;
make us mindful to offer them our help and support;
and guide us to create a world
where each child born is welcomed, loved, and cared for.
In Jesus' name we pray.
Amen.

Blessing a New Baby

Giver of life,
we ask that you bless baby insert name
and newborn babies everywhere.
Guide us to love and care for them;
help them to grow healthy and strong;
and give parents and caregivers patience and rest.
May all babies lead us to remember
that you, O God, became a baby in Jesus, the Christ child,
and you always side with those who are weak, powerless,
and most in need of love.
Amen.

For New Brothers or Sisters

Giver of life, who calls us to be our brother's or sister's keepers,
we thank you for new brothers and sisters,
and we celebrate the bonds between siblings.
Like Miriam and Moses, Peter and Andrew, or Saints Clare and Agnes,
bless them to laugh and play together,
to protect each other and pray together.
May they follow the example of Jesus Christ, our heavenly brother,
and teach one another to love, share, and show kindness.
Amen.

For When a Parent Is Away

Loving God, you came to us in Jesus.
He felt what we feel,
and you know what it feels like to miss someone you love,
to be worried or afraid, or to simply want to be hugged or held.
Give me peace while my (*mom* and/or *dad*) is away;
give me faith that I will see them again soon;
and help me trust that no matter where they are,
their love is always in my heart and soul;
through Jesus Christ our Savior.
Amen.

For Parents' Divorce

God of healing, you are with us in our hardest moments,
especially when our hearts are broken,
when parents separate,
and when we are afraid of what will happen next.
Comfort me with your Spirit of peace;
help me to share what I'm feeling inside with people I trust;
and give me faith that Jesus is with me,
that saints and angels surround me,
and that, no matter what happens,
nothing can ever separate me from your love, O God.
Amen.

For When Someone Moves

God of journeys and new beginnings,
we pray for our friend who is moving.
Help their family to feel at home wherever they go;
give them courage to make new friends and explore new places;
and send your Spirit to give them calm in this season of change.
Be with me, also, when I miss my friends,
and give me the faith that, no matter the distance,
our friendship and love will always keep our souls close together;
Amen.

For When Someone Is Sick

God of mercy and comfort,
as Jesus took care of those who were ill,
please take care of your child, insert name, who is sick.
Give rest and comfort to all who need healing;
give wisdom and patience to caregivers;
guide us to prevent sickness from spreading;
and thank you for the medicine and prayers
that can help cure sickness.
May we always remember this:
when we care for the sick, we are caring for Christ.
In Jesus' name we pray.
Amen.

For When Someone Is Hurting

God who hears our cries,
you feel our deepest pains
and you are with anyone who hurts in mind, body, or spirit.
Be with insert name, in this time of need.
Comfort them with your Holy Spirit;
let the light of Christ shine within them;
and give us your mercy so that we may surround those who are hurting with love and support.
In Jesus' name we pray.
Amen.

For When Someone Is Having a Bad Day

God of love,
Jesus had good and bad days.
You were with him during his worst moments,
and you are with us on our good and bad days.
Help us to feel your presence when things aren't going our way;
please give us comfort and friends to lean on;
and let us remember that you love us, no matter what.
In Jesus' name we pray.
Amen.

For My Community

For Libraries

God of wisdom,
you blessed us with the ability to read,
and you speak to us through poetry, stories, histories, and myths.
We thank you, God, for the libraries
and for the joy and knowledge they provide.
Bless the librarians and staff who run them,
and the children and adults who use them;
may they be centers of imagination and public life; centers of imagination and public life;
and help us to protect and preserve libraries
and to secure the freedom to read for generations to come.
Amen.

For Parks and Playgrounds

God of joy,
you walked with us in the garden of Eden,
and in the park we feel your Spirit in nature.
You made us playful creatures,
and when we play, we feel your pleasure.
We thank you, God, for the parks and playgrounds in our lives,
for the people who use them and for those who keep them safe and clean.
Guide us to make parks and playgrounds available to all,
and help us protect and preserve them for generations to come.
Amen.

For Farmers Markets

God of growth and community,
you bring forth food from the earth,
and give us the wisdom to harvest, collect, and
share it.
We thank you for farmers markets,
and for the chance to support local farmers,
bakers, and vendors.
Bless those who sell their goods,
that they make a living and bring others joy;
bless the customers, that they be generous and kind;
and help us all to be aware of how food is grown, gathered, and sold.
Amen.

For Charities, Food Banks, and Shelters

God of compassion,
who calls us to hunger and thirst for justice,
we thank you for the charities, food banks, shelters,
and all places that serve people in need.
Guide us to do as Christ commanded:
to feed the hungry, welcome the stranger,
and help those who need clothing.
Fill us with your Spirit of love,
so that we may serve our neighbors as friends—
ready to give our attention, time, and money,
and ready to receive the gift of being with others,
united as children of God.
Amen.

For Daycares and Preschools

God of love and learning,
You entered the world as baby Jesus,
who grew in wisdom and size because adults cared for him,
we thank you for the daycares and preschools throughout the world.
Fill them with the joy and excitement of your Spirit,
let them overflow with laughter and song,
and, most of all, bless the children and their caregivers and teachers.
May all the world proclaim in thought, word, and deed
that the kingdom of God belongs to little children.
Amen.

For Schools, Colleges, and Universities

God of wisdom,
in each soul you planted a desire for discovery and a love of learning,
and we give thanks for schools as places where we can grow together
and produce the fruits of love, justice, and knowledge.
Bless our schools, colleges, and universities;
may they be gardens of truth,
where students, teachers, and families
develop curious minds, open hearts,
helping hands, and hopeful voices.
Amen.

For People in Our Common Life

For Farmers and Farmhands

God of all creation, of the sun and the soil
and of all things that grow,
we give thanks for the farmers who tend the earth;
Bless their hands and the harvest,
that communities, and especially the hungry, may be fed.
Bless the farmhands who pick the produce;
may they receive a fair wage for their labors
and justice from their neighbors.
Open the eyes of our hearts to see
that our lives rely on the work of farmers and farmhands.
Amen.

For Coaches and Mentors

God of mentors and youth,
Of Eli and Samuel, Naomi and Ruth,
we give thanks for the coaches and mentors in our lives,
those special role models who sacrifice their time
and invest in the lives of students;
who teach the importance of patience and practice;
and who care more about the type of people we become
than about how perfectly we perform.
Bless coaches and mentors everywhere,
to be examples of integrity and care;
may they inspire us to reach our greatest potential
and share our talents and gifts with others.
Amen.

For Artists

God our creator,
maker of all things bright and beautiful, wise and wonderful,
our universe is your work of art,
and we are creative creatures, made in your image.
Thank you, God, for artists of all ages—
for poets, painters, designers, dancers,
musicians, builders, storytellers, and artists of every kind—
and for the life and joy they add to the world.
Inspire each artist with your Spirit;
bless their practice, hard work, and talent;
and bless their artwork that it draws us closer to the world and you.
Amen.

For City Workers

God who binds community together,
we give thanks for the workers of our cities:
for crossing guards and garbagemen,
for those who care for our parks and public places,
for the people who keep the water and streets clean,
for those who work in child and family services and in housing,
and everyone else who helps us live as better neighbors.
Amen.

For First Responders

God of service and selflessness,
thank you for the people who respond first to emergencies in our world,
those brave men and women who risk their lives for the sake of others:
paramedics, firefighters, rescue teams, the nurses and doctors in the ER, police officers, and ordinary citizens who go out of their way to meet the needs of their neighbors.
Bless them and keep your hand of love over them,
and make us mindful to always express our gratitude for their sacrifice.
Amen.

For Health Care Workers

God of healing,
in Christ you welcomed the sick, brought people back to health,
and commanded us to do the same for
friends and strangers alike.
We give thanks for healthcare workers
everywhere,
for doctors, nurses, medics, therapists,
dentists,
and all who care for others in need of
physical, mental, or spiritual healing;
guide them with your Holy Spirit using modern science, wisdom,
and love; and give them rest to be able to serve with energy and joy.
Amen.

For Courts of Justice

God of fairness,
since ancient times you've guided your people with
judges and laws.
Thank you for the courts around the world that seek to
provide justice.
Give wisdom to all juries, judges, lawyers, clerks,
and all who work in the courts.
Bless them to do their jobs with mercy and
understanding,
always committed to the common good,
and always guided by your command to love your neighbor.
Finally, O God, inspire young people with your Spirit of truth,
to become judges and lawyers, committed to the rights of others,
especially those in greatest need.
Amen.

For Government Leaders

God of all nations,
we pray for the leaders in government.
Guide them to lead with integrity and with love for the public.
Help them to listen to the voices of those who have been left out, hurt, wronged, or denied a voice.
Give them a willingness to find common ground with people with whom they disagree,
a firmness to stand for what is right when under pressure,
and a love for their enemies when it feels impossible.
Most of all, anoint them with your wisdom,
that they may protect the earth and the rights of others for generations to come.
Amen.

For Our Enemies

Almighty God,
your way is the way of love,
even when it seems impossible.
Jesus loved his enemies,
and he commanded us to do the same.
Fill us with the Spirit of Christ,
so that we may love our enemies
and, while always seeking safety,
guide us to pray for those who are unkind to us or hurt us.
Please give us the hope that friendship is always possible;
through Jesus Christ our Lord.
Amen.

COFFEE HOUR every Sunday after the service
BAKE sale!

PART 4

Praying through the Church

As a project, students in my religion class design a cathedral on Minecraft, which is like a digital version of LEGOs. In preparation, we research cathedrals and churches from around the world. It quickly becomes evident that most of these buildings are in the shape of a cross. The people typically sit, stand, and gather exactly where Jesus' body would be on that cross. "It's the architect's way of telling us," I say, "that the people gathered for prayer are the Body of Christ."

"Does that mean I'm Jesus' hand?" asked one child. "That's where I usually sit."

"I'm his head."

"I'm his stomach."

"I prefer being the feet."

Their ideas are not far from Saint Paul's. He describes the Church as the Body of Christ, emphasizing that "the body is not one member, but many." The body only works if the various parts work together towards common goals. As Christ's Body, each church member is valuable, each has a role to play, and each deserves recognition and prayer.

A point I highlight is that while the beauty of cathedrals and churches points to God, what makes something a church is not the building itself. What makes something a church is the faithful followers of Jesus who gather in prayer and holy practices.

The key practices that set churches apart from other communities are called "sacraments." Each sacrament is a unique form of prayer that we see at work in the story of Jesus. By practicing the sacraments, we receive God's loving grace and become part of the story of Christ.

The goal of this section is to pray for the sacraments, for the people at church, and for the holy events that frequently occur when Christians are gathered.

Sacraments

For Baptism

God of new life,
whose love overflows,
and whose justice rolls down like water,
we thank you for the sacrament of baptism,
where you send the Holy Spirit upon us,
forgive us of our sins,
raise us to the new life in Christ,
and mark us as children of God forever.
Guide us to grow in the community of faith,
and lead us deeper into your overflowing love;
through Jesus Christ our Savior.
Amen.

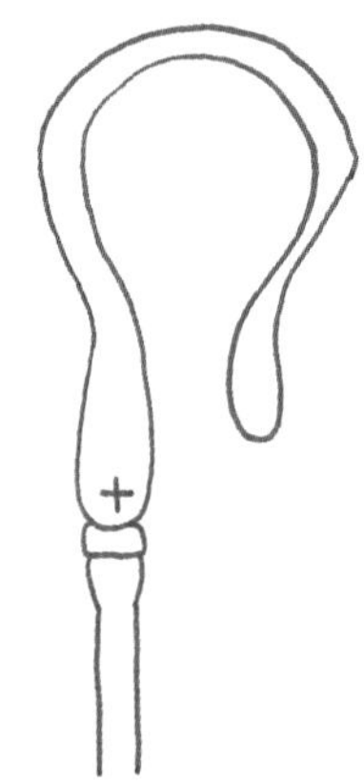

For Confirmation

God of covenants,
in the waters of baptism we were forgiven of sin,
buried with Jesus in his death,
and raised to share in his resurrected life.
We thank you for the sacrament of confirmation,
where we confirm the promises of baptism,
proclaim our faith in public,
recommit ourselves to Jesus Christ,
and receive power from the Holy Spirit
to go in peace to love and serve the Lord.
Amen.

For the Eucharist

God of holy mysteries,
through the miracle of Jesus' birth,
you became one of us,
Son of God made flesh and blood.
We thank you for the sacrament of Holy Communion,
where that miracle continues,
and your holy flesh and blood becomes one with us
in the bread and wine of the Eucharist.
Teach us to receive this spiritual food with faith
that we become part of the Body of Christ,
He in us, and we in Him,
united with all the company of heaven
in thanksgiving to God;
through Jesus Christ our Savior.
Amen.

For Reconciliation

God of mercy,
all of heaven rejoices
when someone who was lost to sin is found
and reunited with the family of God.
We thank you for the sacrament of reconciliation,
when you give us the chance to be set free
from the sins that weigh us down.
Give us the courage to search our hearts,
confess our sins, and ask for forgiveness,
trusting that your love always surrounds us and welcomes us home;
through Jesus Christ our Savior.
Amen.

For Holy Orders

God of the apostles,
through the Holy Spirit, you have called your followers
to play different roles in the Church.
We thank you for the sacrament of holy orders.
Bless deacons in their ministry of service,
especially serving the poor, the weak, the sick, and the lonely.
Bless priests in their ministry of preaching, pastoring,
and practicing the sacraments.
Bless bishops in their ministry of oversight and supervision.
Continue to raise up new clergy for your Church,
and help young people to be open to your call
to become part of the Church's holy orders.
In Jesus' name we pray.
Amen.

For Marriage

Faithful God,
Jesus performed his first miracle at a wedding,
and showed us the joy you take
when two people are united in heart, body, and mind.
We thank you for the sacrament of marriage.
Bless all married couples who have been joined together,
that they comfort, honor, and keep one another.
Bless each marriage that it be for us a mysterious sign
of the love and union between Christ and the Church.
In Jesus' name we pray.
Amen.

For Anointing the Sick

God of healing,
Jesus showed us that you are with us
especially when we are hurting the most or closest to death.
We thank you for the sacrament of anointing the sick,
where your ministers go to those
who need healing of body, mind, or spirit,
and give them grace by laying hands on them in prayer
or marking them with the cross using holy oil.
May the anointing of the sick always remind us
of our responsibility to care for others' physical, mental, and spiritual health.
In Jesus' name we pray.
Amen.

For the People at Church

For Teachers and Students

God of wisdom,
we give thanks for Christians who answer your call to teach,
who draw students closer to you, O God,
through their lessons, through their prayers,
and, most of all, through the example of your love.
Bless the bond between teachers and students;
guide them to continue learning how to follow Jesus;
and give them confidence that through their words and example,
they are planting seeds of faith and transforming the lives of one another;
through Jesus Christ our Savior.
Amen.

For Choristers

God of all creation,
who has done marvelous things,
we give thanks for the choristers who praise you in song,
whose voices carry our prayers to you,
and open our hearts to your harmony and love.
Bless each chorister to grow in faith and skill.
Bless the bonds they share with others in the choir.
And bless the music they make,
that it may draw us closer to ourselves, our neighbors, and you.
May their song join the morning stars to sing your praises,
as we, your children, shout for joy;
through Jesus Christ our Savior.
Amen.

For Music Directors and Instrumentalists

Lord of all hopefulness,
you speak to our souls through music,
and when your Spirit fills our hearts,
we can speak to one another with psalms, hymns, and songs.
We give thanks for the music directors and instrumentalists
who teach us to listen to the holy,
who tune our hearts to the sound of love,
and who lead us to lift our voices in praise.
Bless them and the music they make;
may it transform us and all who hear it,
so that we may transform the world
to the glory of God;
through Jesus Christ our Savior.
Amen.

For Acolytes

Living God,
you desire that we worship you
in the beauty of holiness,
and we give thanks for people
who answer your call to be acolytes,
who help us to form the thoughts of our hearts,
who guide us in giving shape to our prayers,
and who show us how to worship as a team.
Bless all acolytes, that through their service,
they and all who worship with them
discover the joy of Christ,
the unity of the Holy Spirit,
and the love of God.
In Jesus' name we pray.
Amen.

For Ushers and Greeters

God of welcome,
you visited Abraham and Sarah in disguise,
and you blessed them for welcoming you into their home.
We thank you for Christians who answer your call
to show hospitality to all who enter the church.
Bless all greeters and ushers, that they be filled with your Spirit,
that they seek and serve Christ in all persons,
and that they make others feel seen, heard, and appreciated.
May their example be a holy reminder:
when we welcome others, we welcome you.
In Jesus' name we pray.
Amen.

For Altar and Flower Guilds

God of all things bright and beautiful,
you prepare a table before us
and invite us to see how you care for the lilies.
We give thanks for church members
who are called to serve on altar or flower guilds.
Bless them and all who work behind the scenes
quietly preparing what we hold dear.
Bless their ministry of leading others to you.
May their flowers remind us of Easter
when new life bursts forth at the resurrection of Jesus.
May the altar remind us of the invitation
to come to God's table and become part of the Body of Christ.
Let their examples inspire us to use our gifts to serve you.
In Jesus' name we pray.
Amen.

For Sextons

God of all that is seen and unseen,
We recognize the great deal of work
that is required for us to gather at church.
We give thanks for sextons
and for the cleanliness and readiness that they provide.
Make us mindful to not take others' labor for granted;
guide us to treat them with dignity and respect;
and help us to express our gratitude with our words and actions;
through Jesus Christ our Savior.
Amen.

For Elders

Giver of life and Ancient of Days,
We give thanks for our elders,
and we ask for your blessing upon them.
Give them a peace that passes understanding.
Help us to cherish them and the precious time we have together.
Open our hearts to listen to their knowledge and wisdom,
and inspire us to learn their stories.
May their hopes and dreams be carried from generation to generation;
through Jesus Christ our Savior.
Amen.

For Children and Youth

Loving God,
who told us we must become like children to enter your kingdom,
we thank you for every child and youth,
especially those in our church and community.
Bless them with joy and surround them with holy friendships;
give them visions of justice and peace;
and guide them with your Holy Spirit,
that they may follow Jesus in embracing" to simply "embrace
themselves and the world.
Bless our words and actions, that each child and youth
comes to trust that Christ is always with them.
Amen.

For the Vestry

God of wisdom,
you gather us together as a church,
to worship you, support one another, and serve our neighbors.
We thank you for calling each member of the vestry to leadership.
Bless them and the gifts they offer to the church.
Fill them with your Holy Spirit,
that they may work together, pray together, and lead together.
And guide them to further the mission of your kingdom,
by offering their talents, experience, and knowledge,
all to the glory of God.
In Jesus' name we pray.
Amen.

For Godparents

God whose love overflows,
you call loved ones to serve as godparents
to those baptized as children of God.
Bless those who are godparents already
and those who will be godparents soon.
May they always remember their promise
to bring their godchildren up in the Christian faith and way of life;
through their words and actions,
may godparents show what it means to be a follower of Jesus;
and on every anniversary of a godchild's baptism,
may each godparent give a loving reminder
that their godchild is part of God's story of new life in Christ.
In Jesus' name we pray.
Amen.

For Candidates for Baptism

God of living water,
who calls us to die to sin
and to be raised to new life as a child of God,
we thank you for the sacrament of baptism,
and for candidates of all ages
who will be baptized into the Body of Christ.
Anchor forgiveness and hope deep in each heart.
In the souls of all who will be baptized,
give peace like a river, love like an ocean,
and joy like a fountain.
We pray this in the name of Jesus, whose love overflows.
Amen.

For Candidates for Confirmation

God of sacraments,
whose Holy Spirit is bound to all who are baptized
and who marks them as Christ's own forever,
we give thanks for the candidates for confirmation
and for their desire to renew the promises of baptism.
Guide them in heart, soul, mind, and strength,
to continue in the life of the Church,
to renounce evil and proclaim the gospel,
to seek and serve Christ in all persons,
and to strive for justice, peace, and dignity for all humankind;
through Jesus Christ our Savior.
Amen.

For Pilgrims

God of pilgrimage,
You planted a desire in us to seek out what is holy,
and when you speak to us through holy places and practices,
the memory of what you have done comes to life in us,
and we become part of your holy story.
Unite us, through prayer, with all past, present, and future pilgrims.
Bless us to form sacred bonds with those we journey with,
remind us to carry loved ones back home in our hearts,
inspire us to offer a part of ourselves to the places we encounter,
and guide us to take a part of each holy place back home with us.
May the seeds of this pilgrimage lead to self-discovery,
leaving each of us transformed by the love of the Holy One.
Amen.

For the Events at Church

Bible Studies

Living God,
who speaks through scripture and
tradition, reason and experience,
bless each Bible study and let it be an act
of prayer.
Help us to listen with open hearts.
Guide us to read responsibly and through
a lens of love.
Inspire us to bring ourselves, our stories, and our intellect
to our study.
Most of all, like the disciples on the road to Emmaus,
set our hearts on fire and let this Bible study reveal
that you are in the midst of our fellowship and learning;
through Jesus Christ our Savior.
Amen.

For Coffee Hour

God of fellowship,
we give thanks for coffee hour
and for the times at church when we set aside time
to enjoy the presence of one another.
Bless coffee hour and similar occasions.
Send your Holy Spirit to dwell with us,
so that strangers are welcomed,
friendships are forged and strengthened,
the bonds between young and old are increased,
and the lives of churchgoers be renewed
through joy, laughter, and delicious snacks.
In Jesus' name we pray.
Amen.

For Potlucks

God of plenty,
we give thanks for church potlucks,
those events when each person gets to share their food
and eat from the food shared by others.
Bless our meal to be a sign of your kingdom,
where all are welcomed, fed, and eat from a common table.
May this potluck train our hearts
to share not just food but our whole lives;
through Jesus Christ our Savior.
Amen.

For Feeding the Hungry

Lord Jesus,
you are the Bread of Life who shares yourself with us
and commands us to feed the hungry.
In a world where plenty is possible,
inspire our hearts with compassion and joy
to provide food to all who hunger
and to engage them in fellowship.
Give us eyes of faith to seek and serve Christ in all persons
and respect the dignity of every human being.
Finally, guide us not only to feed the hungry,
but to also ask why they are hungry and seek long-term
solutions.
Amen.

For Marching for Justice

God of the oppressed,
you have commanded us to do justice,
love kindness, and walk humbly with you.
Please bless us with the courage to pray with our feet
by standing against sin and marching for justice.
Give us the confidence that Christ walks with us,
empower us with your Spirit when we're afraid or threatened,
and allow our steps and voices to be a testimony
to justice, peace, and the dignity of every human being;
through Jesus Christ our Savior.
Amen.

For Donation Drives

God of charity,
all things belong to you,
and all blessings are meant to be shared.
Help us to embrace opportunities to give to others,
to open our hearts and hands,
and to offer our donations joyfully.
As we give to those in need,
let us seek to understand their needs,
to celebrate them as children of God,
and to have faith in a future where all needs are met.
Amen.

For a Mission Trip

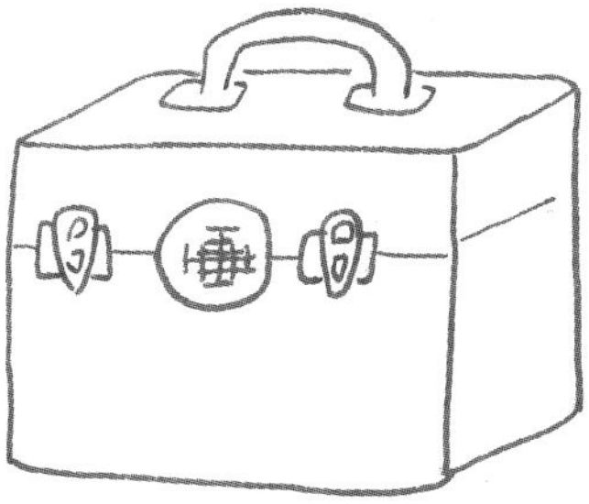

God of service,
who calls us to humbly serve others,
we thank you for the opportunity
to make a difference in the world
and to be transformed.
Bless this mission trip as we journey together,
guide us to be aware of our privilege,
knit our lives together as a group,

and help us to approach those we serve as equals,
with faith that we are brothers and sisters in Christ.
In Jesus' name we pray.
Amen.

For a Parish Retreat

God of fellowship and rest,
as Jesus often took breaks to be alone with his disciples,
we also pause from our busy lives
to pray, relax, and enjoy the company of our congregation.
Bless our time together, and breathe your Holy Spirit upon us,
to renew our spirits,
to strengthen our friendships,
and to deepen our love for you, one another, and our church;
through Jesus Christ our savior and friend.
Amen.

PART 5
Praying with Creation

"Daddy, guess what?" my daughter said. "I saw God today."

"Where did you see God?" I replied.

"In the sky."

"Wow! What did God look like?" I asked.

"God didn't have a body. I saw God in the sky."

"Oh, you mean like the clouds, the sunshine, the fog?"

"Yes!"

"How did you know God was there?"

"I felt this peace, and it was like I was protected, like everything is going to be okay."

My earliest memory of a spiritual or religious experience occurred when I was five years old. I was lying beneath a maple tree, gazing up at the sky. Resting on the grass in that moment of grace, a kind of divine peace washed over me, welled up within me. I encountered a mystery that I eventually came to know as God.

My daughter's experience and the memory of my own encounter with God in nature reminded me that children naturally have a holy connection to nature.

On the Feast Day of Saint Francis, I was outside teaching kindergartners, and we were doing what I call a "walking prayer," where we pray using walking instead of words. As we were leaving, one boy said, "That made me feel like Saint Francis. It's easy to pray when you're outside."

"This is true," I told him. It's also true that the older you get, the more challenging it becomes to pray outside—or anywhere, for that matter. Worries, stress, deadlines, distractions—all pull us away from God's glory, which surrounds us in the natural world and shines deep within our souls. Nature is a dwelling for God's presence. God is the mystery of love and the heartbeat of creation. This section is intended to help us listen to and embrace creation as our partner in prayer.

Thanksgivings and Blessings

For the Beauty of Outer Space

God of the heavens,
whose words formed the universe,
and whose Love moves the sun and the other stars,
we praise you for the beauty of outer space:
from our swirling Milky Way
to the furthest-stretching cosmic ray;
for each eclipse and constellation,
for supernovas and space stations,
your glory shines in all directions.
Open our hearts to the song of the morning stars,
and may the beauty of interstellar life
give us a deeper reverence for creation,
especially life on Earth, our fragile home.
Amen.

For the Beauty of the Earth

Tender God,
whose hands have molded the dry land
and shaped the heights of the hills,
we praise you for the beauty of the Earth:
from deserts with their sandy waves
to plains, volcanos, reefs, and caves;
for each beach and river running wide,
each jungle buzzing full of life.
Open our hearts to the chorus of the mountains that sings for joy;
may the beauty of the Earth
give us a deeper reverence for all creation.
Amen.

For the Beauty of Plant Life

God of all seasons, gardener of resurrection,
who planted the tree of life in Eden
and makes all things grow,
we praise you for the beauty of plant life:
from the tender grapes that cover the vine
to flowering fields and forests so high;
for each seed, spore, and blossom,
each root, stem, and fruit.
Open our hearts to hear all the trees of the wood rejoice,
and guide us to see heaven in a wild flower.
May the patient wisdom of plants
give us a deeper reverence for all creation.
Amen.

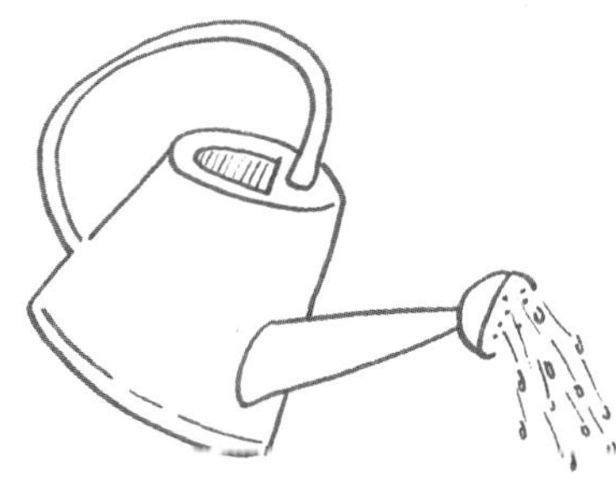

For the Beauty of Water

God of living water, fountain of life,
whose Spirit hovered over the deep
and who offers new life in the waters of baptism,
we praise you for the beauty of water:
from the glaciers that hold our climate in balance
to the water that makes up over half the human body;
for each ocean, lake, and pond,
each waterfall and stream.
Open our hearts to hear how the seas have lifted
their voice of pounding waves in a song of praise.
May the beauty of water wash over us
and give us a deeper reverence for all creation.
Amen.

For the Beauty of All Creatures

Maker of all things bright and beautiful,
we praise you for the beauty and diversity
of all creatures great and small:
from the graceful blue whales and hawks high above
to butterflies, bees, and the pets we love;
for each lion and lamb, each dove and each dog,
each platypus and snake, each fox and hedgehog.
Open our hearts to hear how
all living creatures give glory and thanks to you.
May the beauty of all creatures
give us a deeper reverence for all creation.
Amen.

For the Beauty of Human Responsibility

God of nature and freedom,
we thank you for blessing humans with the responsibility
to treat the earth as your temple
and to love all the creatures that you have made.
Help us to respond with reverence
towards everything you have created:
to kiss the earth and love it, tirelessly;
to join the prayer and praise of the natural world;
and to see Christ at the heart of creation.
Bless our actions to show that all life is inter-connected,
and that all are responsible for all.
In Jesus' name we pray.
Amen.

For the Sabbath Rest

God who renews all life,
you command us to pause each week
so that we can rest in the beauty of creation
and spend time with you,
free from work and busyness,

free from consumption and comparison,
free to worship with our community
and be together with the people we love.
Give us the discipline to take a sabbath rest each week,
to demand a pause for our lives and for the natural world.
Amen.

For Addressing the Climate Crisis

God of justice,
you intend for all creation to grow, thrive, and multiply,
and you see the emergency of the climate crisis
threatening your environment and all the life that it holds in balance.
Empower us with your Spirit of truth,
to take responsibility for finding solutions;
give us the courage of Christ
to take a stand against the powers of destruction;
and bless us with a willingness to make the sacrifices necessary
to protect and preserve our environment for generations to come.
Amen.

Blessing of a Bird Nest

We thank you, God, for birds;
for the melody of their songs
that praise your holy name;
for the beauty of their wings
that lift our eyes to heaven;
and, here, in this moment,
we bless this bird nest,
which houses young eggs or baby birds.
May our own homes, like this nest,
be places where our souls
will grow in song, learn to fly,
and add to the glory
of this wonderful world.
Amen.

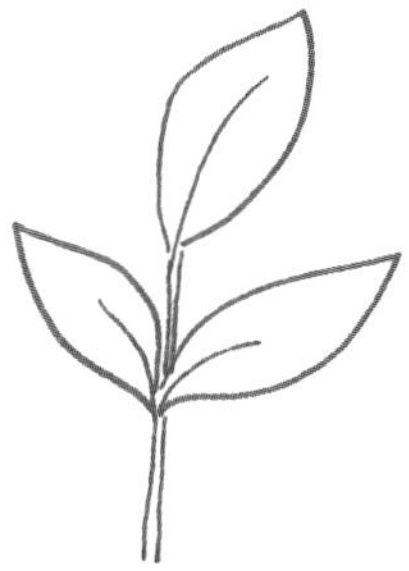

Blessing of a Sunrise

Dazzling and tremendous God,
looking east on this new day,
we bless the sunrise.
May each rising of the sun
be a reminder of the eternal Easter morning,
when your Son, Jesus Christ,
rose in glory from death to new life.
Be present in each ray of sunlight
that meets us today,
and unlock the power of Christ within each of us,
to become a sunrise,
shining the light and love of the Son of God
on everyone we meet.
Amen.

Blessing of a Sunset

God of glory and rest,
with our eyes facing west,
we bless the sunset as this day now ends.
May the glowing gold, citrus, and purple shades of the dusk
remind us of the many colors of your love.
Let our hearts and minds be swept
into that heavenly sky where the sun descends,
reminding us that the light of your Son, Jesus Christ,
dwells in us both day and night,
and speaks to us through the beauty of creation.
Amen.

For Creation

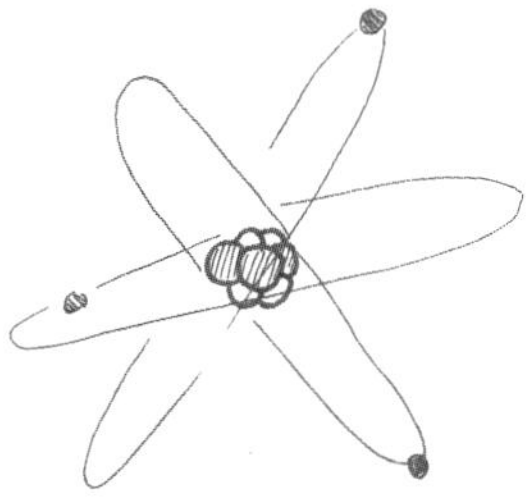

For Knowledge of God's Creation

God of all creation,
like Adam in the garden of Eden
naming every living creature,
you plant in each soul
the desire to understand and know
your glorious world, and how it works and grows.
Guide us with your Holy Spirit,
to follow the truth, wherever it may lead;
to seek knowledge for the sake of wisdom over wealth;
and to bless what we've learned
to spread goodness and health;
through Jesus Christ our Savior.
Amen.

For Sustainable Living

God of all hopefulness,
You created us to live in harmony with the world,
so that our actions and impact
keep the balance of life intact:
Air and water and soil that's clean,
waste that decomposes when it's unseen.
Please give us faith to act sustainably,
to discover the freedom of living simply,
taking no more than we need,
working and consuming at a nourishing speed.
With your power working in us, give us the confidence
that we will make a lasting difference in the end.
Amen.

For Endangered and Extinct Species

God of the living and the dead, we pause and pray
for the glorious creatures that you once made
that were brought to extinction
because of human selfishness and greed.
May we honor the lives of those species now extinct
by committing ourselves to the protection
of endangered species and life that's threatened.
We repent of the destruction that humanity has done,
and we live with hope in the risen Christ
that someday the world may live as one.
Amen.

For the Future of Humankind

Eternal God,
we pray for the future of humankind,
and when we are worried
or afraid of what is to come,
we remember what you, through Christ, have done:
You became one of us in Mary's womb,
defeated death with love in an empty tomb,
and sent your Holy Spirit to fill us with power,
to transform the world in its darkest hours.
United with you in each crisis we face,
we look to our future with trust in your grace.
In Jesus' name we pray.
Amen.

For the Care of Creation

For Recycling and Composting

God of all creation,
who desires that nothing be put to waste
and commands us to care for the earth,
guide us to recycle and compost as forms of prayer;
please give us your heavenly willpower
to resist the temptation of single-use containers and materials;
inspire us to invent new ways of recycling
and to discover new uses for composting;
and when we have done what is good for the environment,
help us to feel the joy of your Spirit.
Amen.

For Eating Mindfully

God of gratitude,
who prepares a table for us
and meets us in a meal with bread and wine,
please give us the patience to eat mindfully:
mindful of the earth that provides the food,
mindful of the hands that prepare and serve it,
mindful of the flavors and conversations we share,
mindful of Christ's presence in those gathered with us.
In all that we do, and in every meal,
give us the mind of Christ.
Amen.

For Traveling Mindfully

God of all mindfulness,
you are with us everywhere,
in every journey and destination,
in every dream and meditation.
Please guide us with your Holy Spirit
to travel mindfully,
whether we're going near or far.
Give us an awareness of our surroundings,
help us to be grateful for the people we pass,
and move us to make choices that respect the environment
and reduce our carbon footprint.

For Sharing the Earth's Resources

Generous God,
who blessed the earth with enough resources
for all humanity to share and grow together,
empty our hearts of the desire to own and control,
open our hands to give to all who are in need,
focus our minds with the wisdom to take no more than we need,
and guide us to bring those who misuse resources to justice.
May we only act in a renewable manner,
for the sake of generations to come.
Amen.

For Those Most Affected by Climate Change

God of compassion,
whose Spirit moans with the cries of creation,
you hear the cries and fears
of those most affected by climate change.
Comfort them with your Holy Spirit,
strengthen them with a hope for justice,
discomfort those who do nothing to help,
and judge the actions of the people and nations
who are most responsible for the climate crisis.

We pray this in the name of Jesus,
who taught us that, with you, O God,
all things are possible.
Amen.

For Those Who Lack Clean Air, Water, or Other Necessities

Caring God,
on the cross Jesus gasped for air,
went through the agony of thirst,
and showed us that you take the side of all who suffer.
We pray for those who lack clean air, clean water,
and other necessities to live.
Help us to comfort and protect them in their suffering;
guide us to give our time, talents, and resources,
so that they may live in safety and receive justice;
and fill our world with the wisdom and courage
to reject practices of environmental destruction
and embrace a clean creation.
Amen.

For Those Who Strive for Environmental Justice

Steadfast God,
you blessed Noah and his family
because they were just and righteous,
working to save what you had made
amid a culture of violence.
At a time when the earth suffers because of human actions,
we ask you to bless all who strive for environmental justice:
empower their words and actions to inspire change,
give them the confidence when they are ignored or ridiculed,
and unite them with justice seekers of every kind.
May their example teach each of us that we have a role
and responsibility in the balance of creation.
Amen.

ABOUT THE ILLUSTRATIONS

The ink drawings in this prayer book are intended to invite children and families into the scenes through details and characters. The images depict a community of animals who live and worship together in community throughout the year and in and out of an average day. These pictures represent the many ways and reasons we pray and the potential to encounter saints and holiness in each day, even in the ordinary things we do. Prayer can happen anywhere and look like many things. You can pray by yourself or with friends and family.

Perry Hodgkins Jones works for a clean energy consulting firm by day and is an illustrator by night. She grew up in New Jersey and now lives in Alexandria, VA, at Episcopal High School with her spouse, child, and sleepy cat. Perry is a graduate of Wellesley College and the School of Theology at the University of the South in Sewanee, where she received an M.A. in Religion and the Environment.